GAIJIN SHOGUN

General Douglas A. MacArthur
Stepfather of Postwar Japan

Gaijin Shogun
General Douglas MacArthur

David J. Valley

Illustrated with period photographs

The Sektor Company, San Diego, California

i

Gaijin Shogun
General Douglas A. MacArthur
Stepfather of Postwar Japan

Published by The Sektor Company
P.O. Box 501005
San Diego, California 92150, U.S.A.

Copyright © 2000 by David J. Valley
Library of Congress Catalog Card Number: 99-91941

Publisher's Cataloging-in-Publication
Valley, David J.

Author's email: dvalley@fda.net
Gaijin Shogun—General Douglas A. Macarthur—
Stepfather of Postwar Japan/David J. Valley. —1st ed.

Includes illustrations and bibliographical references.

ISBN: 0-9678175-2-8

TABLE
OF CONTENTS

ILLUSTRATIONS

ACKNOWLEDGMENTS

This book sets the stage for a commemorative project to honor Gen. Douglas MacArthur and all who served in the Occupation on the fiftieth anniversary of his departure from Japan, April 2001. We are grateful to sponsors and donors supporting this project.

Special thanks to The General MacArthur Foundation for its permission to reprint a portion of the General's autobiographical book, <u>Reminiscences</u>, which is the central core of Gaijin Shogun. The Foundation operates the General MacArthur Memorial in Norfolk, Virginia, a treasure trove of information and memorabilia of the General. I also wish to thank authors and their representatives for other writings used.

Thanks to friends who helped to review, edit and make suggestions for improving the book, along with their general encouragement. I am especially grateful to James Yoshida, who provided a Japanese perspective, and to fellow Honor Guard members Rod Bechtel, Bob Johnson and Maurice Howe for their support. I wish to thank Sandra Burns for corrections, and Hugh Crumpler for his thoughtful review and kind words.

Special recognition goes to that person in my life, my wife Dottie, who by her unfailing support, encouragement, and guidance keeps me on an even keel and takes care of so many things, allowing me the time and peace of mind to pursue my hobbies.

David Valley

FOREWORD

This book is a compilation of the works of others along with writings by the author to provide overviews of the period and to elaborate on certain points. The heart of the book is from General MacArthur's autobiographical work, <u>Reminiscences</u>. Portions are reprinted with the permission of the Gen. MacArthur Foundation, which has also been helpful in the collection of photographs shown in this book.

Contributions by writers other than the author are indicated by a vertical bar. When these writers quote from another source, separate indentations are used. Chapter IV is primarily comprised of writings by General MacArthur. Contributions by David Valley and other writers are enclosed in boxes.

Pictures are dispersed throughout the text, roughly in the vicinity of a related subject. Knowing that some readers may only skim and look at pictures, the photographs and detailed captions attempt to convey the essence of the story. All captions are by the author.

Although this book is based on factual events and accurate reproduction of the writings of others, the intent, in its entirety is to tell an interesting story, rather than to create a treatise of scholastic merit; my apologies to the academics.

The book's title, <u>Gaijin Shogun, Gen. Douglas A. MacArthur, Stepfather of Postwar Japan</u>, is meant to convey the theme of the book while being a bit provocative. To most Americans the title might be taken at face value or passed over with little thought, to some Japanese the reaction might range from curious to contentious. For those that question the title's validity, a review is in order to ask if the book answers to the title.

'Gaijin Shogun' may be considered a stretch by some, but strictly translated as foreign military ruler, it defines General MacArthur's role in Japan. It is likely the way many Japanese thought of him and the kind of unique and exalted title that might have pleased the General.

Early in the book it is pointed out that neither the Emperor, other Japanese leaders, nor traditional fathers were fully functional at the close of the war. As to calling the General 'stepfather,' the appellation seems appropriate as the term is used to denote a non-natural father who has taken over fatherly duties.

As to 'father,' was the General seen as a father figure? This can be measured by what defines a father, such mutual respect and affection, and a passion to care for and protect. The Japanese people, from the Emperor down, respected the General and most held him in affection. The General also had a deep respect and affection for the Japanese. As to 'a passion to care for and protect,' the book has abundantly made the case that Gen. MacArthur was dedicated to the care, protection, and future welfare of the Japanese people. Such was the entire purpose and focus of his Occupation policies, beyond undoing any future military threat.

I
INTRODUCTION

This book has been compiled from various sources, both American and Japanese, to tell a story that has been forgotten, confused, or maligned. It is written for the young people of Japan, those too young to have experienced their country's misadventure of WWII and the struggle for survival thereafter. It is written for older Japanese, who may have witnessed these events and have their own experiences of personal tribulations, but can neither recall nor envision the larger picture of events that overcame them. It is also written for Americans, especially those who played some part in the rebuilding of Japan whether large or small, that they might remember and be proud of their endeavors and of a country that had the generosity and right-minded spirit to help a people who for a period of time had caused them untold harm. Last, but of deep significance, it is written for the legacy of a man who transcended the bounds of human limitations to lead his country to victory in a brutal war and then pick up the pieces of a broken enemy nation, restoring it to freedom, health, and prosperity.

General Douglas A. MacArthur can rightfully be called the step-father of modern Japan. When most of the fathers of Japan were still returning from distant battlefields, looking for the remnants of their families, wandering around an unrecognizable homeland, scrounging for survival, or in a half-numb state struggling to rebuild, there was only one person in Japan who could bring order from the chaos and make life livable again. It was not the Emperor, who was shorn of his divinity and authority, or any other Japanese leader. All were at the mercy of the Supreme Commander of Allied Powers.

The Supreme Commander's authority came down from the Potsdam Proclamation, the conclave of Allied Powers, United States of America, the United Kingdom, China, Soviet Union, Canada, France, New Zealand and Australia, who joined forces to defeat Germany and Japan. His orders were simple: dismantle the Japanese military, punish those who were guilty, and restore a peaceful order.

1. Reign of shoguns. The term shogun originally meant great military leader. It was first adopted by Minamoto Yoritomo (insert) at the end of the 12th century to designate himself military ruler of all Japan. The shogunate resulted from a power vacuum when the Emperor lacked the military might to rule. The last of the line of shoguns, Tokugawa Keiki (pictured above), ruled until the Meiji Restoration (1867). Then, in 1945, after a brutal war and the unconditional surrender of Japan came the Gaijin Shogun, Gen. Douglas MacArthur.

The task of disarmament and punishment of the guilty was relatively easy; the later task was monumental. If there are times in the course of human events that a divine plan is at work, surely that was the case when a unique personage, Douglas Arthur MacArthur, took on this staggering task.

The stage was set. The Throne was in submission. The masses were confused and suffering. The Gaijin Shojun, sitting in a modest office on the sixth floor of the Dai Ichi building across the avenue from the Imperial Palace grounds, was poised to remake a nation. Should there be any doubt about General MacArthur's omnipotence, consider what the noted historian and Asian expert John Gunther wrote in 1951.

> MacArthur is not head of state (the Emperor is) but he assumes functions of a head of state. The government of Japan has, for instance, no relations whatsoever with the outside world except through the Supreme Commander Allied Powers (SCAP). A foreign diplomat assigned to Tokyo is accredited, not to the Emperor, but to SCAP, and it is MacArthur not the Emperor, who receives ambassadors, heads of missions, and the like. He is a kind of baby sitter for the entire nation.

> In blunt fact MacArthur's authority is so great and his powers so sweeping that he is the actual ruler of Japan. The manner of this rule is often indirect, and a semitransparent facade is carefully maintained behind which Japanese authority is exerted in many fields, but MacArthur is in fact the all powerful boss of 83,000,000 Japanese, and will remain so until a peace treaty is signed.

> Powers of this formidable nature are unique in American history and it is a tribute to MacArthur that he has used them with such moderation.[1]

---

[1] John Gunther, The Riddle of MacArthur, Harper & Brothers, New York, 1951, pp. 15-16

2. Douglas MacArthur as a West Point cadet (1900). The MacArthur family came from prominent Scottish forebearers. Arthur, the grandfather of Douglas, came to America as a young boy and finished his career as a respected U.S. Supreme Court Justice. Douglas's father, Arthur, was a distinguished high ranking army general. Douglas set new records at West Point for his scholarship and leadership. He graduated first in the class of 1903. He returned to West Point in 1919 as a young one-star general and hero of WWI. With characteristic vigor and insight, he restored the faltering institution once more to prominence as the greatest military academy in the world.

(Photo courtesy of U.S. Military Academy Archives)

II
DOUGLAS A. MACARTHUR'S EARLY YEARS

The MacArthur family first came to the shores of America in 1825 when Arthur, the grandfather of Douglas, arrived at the tender age of ten with his widowed mother from Glasgow, Scotland. The family traces its Scottish ancestry back to Medieval times when the MacArthurs (Gaelic - MacArtair) were even then a family of prominence. Arthur's mother must have been a person of some means also, as young Arthur received a first rate formal education, graduating from Amherst College and later passing the Massachusetts Bar. Later he married and his wife gave birth to Arthur, Jr., about the time he had gotten into politics in the State of Wisconsin, where he later became governor. After this stint he decided to make his career in the justice system and was elected to a state judgeship. After the Civil War, President Grant recognized his talent and integrity and appointed him to the U.S. Supreme Court where he served with distinction for twenty years.

During this time, his son Arthur, Jr., was establishing an outstanding reputation of his own as a military leader. As a dashing young captain in the army he won the favor of a southern belle from Norfolk, Virginia (now home of the General MacArthur Memorial), Mary "Pinky" Hardy. "Pinky," as she was well known, was a spunky, strong-minded young lady who was destined to mold one of America's great leaders. She withstood the rigors of army life at remote outposts in the west and dedicated herself to her husband and newborn, Douglas Arthur MacArthur. Douglas was born at Little Rock, Arkansas, on January 26, 1880, where his father was on post at the time.

The MacArthur talent and energy paid off with promotions and assignments of greater responsibility. He had demonstrated his bravery and leadership in several engagements during the Civil War, winning the nation's highest award, the Congressional Medal of Honor. He was severely wounded several times but yet had a total disregard for his personal safety while in battle. Years later Douglas shows the same traits on the battlefield and would also be awarded the Congressional Medal of Honor.

Never before or since has a father and son been so honored.

In many ways, General Arthur MacArthur's life was a precursor for his son's. In the late 1890s, Arthur lead American troops in the Philippines, defeating the Spanish forces that had established sovereignty there for decades. After the Spanish left, however, a large guerrilla force showed great determination to take control of the islands. In a master stroke, General Arthur MacArthur captured the leader of the native forces and convinced him to surrender his army and sign a peace treaty with the U.S. Later his enlightened policies won the hearts of Filipinos and set the stage for their long term devotion to the MacArthur family.

While father was off on foreign soil, Pinky was at home grooming Douglas for greatness. Once he expressed an interest in following her husband's footsteps into the army, she dissuaded him from enlisting and set his sights on obtaining an appointment to West Point, which had to be secured through a sponsoring congressman. The competition was fierce for the few appointments available, which were decided on the basis of academic testing. With Pinky's coaching, Douglas achieved the highest grade and received the appointment.

Undeterred by what others might think, Pinky virtually went to West Point with Douglas, taking an apartment at the Thayer Hotel, just across the street from his dormitory. Her constant involvement seemed to have had a positive effect on the young cadet, as he took on academy life to the fullest. Douglas had a powerful bond with his mother and thrived in her presence. He unleashed an unquenchable thirst for knowledge and scored record high academic marks, at the same time he was very active in sports, playing baseball, football and tennis with better than average skill. He graduated at the head of his class on June 11, 1903, and, because of his high grades, was assigned to the Army Engineers.

His first field assignment was to construct a barracks facility at Leyte in the Philippines. Ironically, he would use these facilities forty years later during WWII. Later he teamed up as an aide to his father, General Arthur MacArthur, who was assigned by Teddy Roosevelt to observe the Russo-Japanese War (1904-1905). This assignment took them to Tokyo where they met all the great Japanese commanders of their day, Oyama, Kuroki, Nogi, and Togo, all of whom made a great impression on young Lt. Douglas MacArthur.

WWI presented the first opportunity for Douglas to hold a major position of combat command. He came to France in 1917 with the Rainbow Division and won every medal the army had for bravery.

He was twice wounded, but like his father, in repeated exposures, defied the enemy to take him down. He rose to the rank of brigadier general and later took command of the division. Interestingly, years later one of his minor officers, a Captain Harry S Truman, would play an important role in the General's waning career.

After the war he took on the most prestigious posts the army had to offer, Superintendent of West Point and Army Chief of Staff. He also served brief tours in the Philippines between 1923 and 1928. For a time before WWII, he was on inactive status but recalled to duty by President Franklin Roosevelt on July 26, 1945, about five months before the fateful attack on Pearl Harbor.

We would be remiss to neglect the General's personal life during these times. Though he was very close to his mother, he was no mama's boy. He was strongly heterosexual and had some notable love affairs. One resulted in his first marriage to a *bon vivant* socialite that ended in divorce after two years of 'army life' which was too rigorous and unappealing to her. By the mid-thirties, during Douglas's assignment in Washington, he kept a devoted Eurasian 'friend' in the Hotel Chastleton; his mother, Pinky, would have been scandalized had she known.

His marriage to the love of his life, the lovely Jean Marie Faircloth, took place some time later, in 1937. She became the ideal mate for this powerful and complex man and, by all measures, he was deeply in love with her and depended on her as his closest confidant.

Though Douglas had achieved great success in his army career, he was never completely comfortable with the civilian authorities. In part this was due to what he perceived as political abuse which thwarted his father's military career, cutting him short of achieving the highest regarded position of Chief of Staff. This may account for Douglas's willingness to take on duties at posts far from Washington, where he could exert his authority with little interference. Ultimately, it may have been the complicating or causative factor in his estrangement from the Truman Administration.

3. Japanese attack Pearl Harbor. On December 7, 1941, Japanese forces launched a brutal surprise attack on the fleet at Pearl Harbor, Hawaii. Caught unprepared, thousands of service personnel and civilians lost their lives as the U.S. fleet was decimated. The U.S.S. Arizona, above, goes to a watery grave, taking over 1200 sailors with her. The site is now a national monument visited every year by thousands of Japanese and American tourists.

Today, it is hard to imagine that a large fleet could sail across the Pacific, within striking distance of Pearl Harbor, and not be detected. At the time there was no long range surveillance other than patrol ships and aircraft, which were not deployed in the crucial area. Ships were clustered in the harbor as Americans were complacent about the possibility of an enemy attack; we paid a great price for that mistake.

III
DAY OF INFAMY

It began many years earlier, when Japan's expansionist policies, exploited by an aggressive military, found helpless victims practically at their doorstep, in Manchuria and Korea. As propaganda shaped the national consciousness, and the military increased its armaments and control over civil authorities, the mis-adventure became wider in scope, into Formosa, China, Singapore, and New Guinea. Easy victories deluded Japanese leaders and the populace into believing in their conjured divine mission and invincibility. Their chartered course was leading them inexorably into a collision with the major power of the Pacific, the United States of America. A few years earlier this prospect would have been unthinkable, but they were now victims of the self-delusion fed to the masses. They readily believed their cause was just and that they had the capability to take on a major power.

Like an eruption of a nest of angry hornets, Japan's finest warriors, hyped-up with fanatical fervor, spewed out their poison and destruction against servicemen and civilians who were relaxing on their traditional day of worship and fellowship. This "Day of Infamy" was December 7, 1945. The place was Pearl Harbor, Hawaii.

Thousands of Americans died in the initial assault; more than 1200 were trapped in the battleship Arizona, which sank in minutes after a bomb pierced its hull and detonated the ship's magazine.

The blow to the Pacific Fleet was devastating as sixty percent of the armada was either sunk or badly damaged. But the loss of lives and materiel was insignificant compared to the unleashed enmity of the American people. Almost overnight a populace of 125 million people began to hate the "Japs," a people they previously knew little or nothing about. Hate unleashed by millions of people is awesome, frightful, and a terrible waste of humankind's purpose. From that day December 7, 1941, millions of innocent lives and countless suffering would accrue as two great nations wasted their most precious assets, their youth and their best leaders.

4. Emperor conducts military review. Emperor Hirohito, in full dress regalia and on his favorite mount, reviews his troops. The '30s and early '40s were heady times for Japanese military and political rulers. The populace was also caught up in the euphoria of the victors and convinced by an unending stream of propaganda that Japan, in pursuit of its divine destiny, was invincible.

Japanese troops were better trained, more aggressive and more dedicated to winning their cause than any armies Americans had met before. Their fervor was roundly described as fanatical, which made it easier to account for their drive, as if they were crazy people. Later it would be understood that the bond between the Japanese fighting men and their Emperor was very special, better understood as a religious and filial dedication than blind fanaticism. This bond made for a formidable foe.

It took over two years for the Americans to recover from the initial assault and subsequent victories by Imperial Forces, but this country has a capacity to invent, develop and mobilize better and faster than any country in the world. This was not entirely evident in the early days of the war, but the spirit of the American people to win, no matter what the odds, fueled by their burning hate for what Japan had done, energized the nation.

The Fleet was rebuilt at a record pace, along with thousands of fighter aircraft, bombers, artillery pieces and personal weapons. The American machine churned them out in an unending stream.

By the hundreds of thousands, airmen, soldiers, sailors and marines paid the price with their lives and suffering for the misdeeds of an errant nation at Bataan, Corregidor, Guadalcanal, Iwo Jima and too many other killing places thousands of miles from their cherished homelands. The reader may find it difficult to relate to statistics of great numbers of casualties and deaths, but the thought of just one lone young soldier, lying in a pool of his own blood with a gaping fatal wound, crying "Mama" in his dying breath, should be enough to convince anyone of the horrors of war.

Besides "slugging it out," there were many strategic victories won by the Allies. Individuals or small groups often had great impact on the course of the war. Heroes known and unknown arose to the occasion as needed. When American forces were within air range of Japan, Col. Jimmy Doolittle launched a one-way bombing attack over Tokyo, the capital of Japan. These brave pilots and crews had barely enough fuel

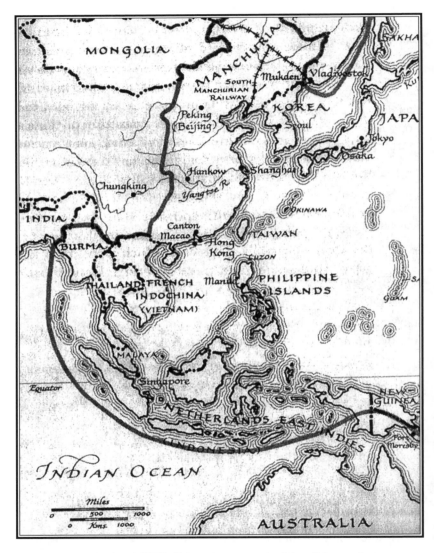

5. Japanese empire - **1943.** Driven by expansionist policies and an aggressive military, Japan invaded neighboring countries of Manchuria and Korea in the '30s. Buoyed by successes, Imperial forces went further afield, under the guise of the Co-Prosperity Policy, into Formosa, China, Singapore and New Guinea. From New Guinea, they were within striking range of Australia, the last stronghold of Allied troops in the Pacific.

to reach Japan and hopefully a little reserve to reach the coast of China after dropping their bombs. Although not causing much damage, the attack was a great morale booster for the Allies. To the Japanese, it was a mighty shock and insult to their invincibility, marking the very first time in the history of Japan that an enemy had breached the sanctity of their homeland.

Another breakthrough that took place without fanfare was the deciphering of the Japanese intelligence code, allowing Allies to intercept and understand all Japanese radio transmissions. This was accomplished by a small group of technicians that today would be likened to computer nerds. A signal event resulting from this coup was information about the air travel of the Japanese naval leader, Admiral Yamamoto. His plane was intercepted by U.S. fighter planes and shot down over the Pacific.

On the other side, the hard work, ingenuity, and skills of the Japanese to produce a massive and effective arsenal and to muster a military of dedicated and competent fighters was being stretched to the limit of the resources within their small island homeland. No longer could the necessities for the war machine, or even for sustaining the populace, be augmented from outside sources. Desperate times led to even more desperate measures, such as the dreaded Kamikaze, where young Japanese, often as young as sixteen and seventeen, willingly submitted to die in suicidal attacks against the enemy.

After major naval battles, such as that at Midway, the Japanese naval armada was fatally weakened, while ground forces were losing battle after battle against refreshed Allied troops coming out of Australia, led by General MacArthur. By late summer 1945 the Allied Forces with their greater resources and leadership prevailed. The Imperial threat was totally crushed. Now all that remained was to take the battle to where the enemy lived, to a country that was already battered to near worthlessness, with a people struggling for survival and thoroughly confused and bewildered by the fast changing events.

As Japanese war leaders recognized the hopelessness of their situation, they drove the people even harder with stories of the atrocities they would suffer should their enemy prevail.

The stage was set for the final days of the war and the surrender of Japan at the Potsdam Conference of Allied Powers on July 26, 1945. As directed by Roosevelt, Churchill, and Stalin, the Potsdam Declaration called for the unconditional surrender of Japan. Though the Japanese government was fully aware by this time of the futility of carrying on the war, many hard core militarists resisted the notion of surrender.

Meanwhile, U.S. Pacific forces under General MacArthur were making plans for the invasion of Japan with a superior military force. By early August all resources currently in the Pacific theater were being readied for the invasion of Kyushu, and plans were underway to bring the U.S. 8th and 1st Armies from Europe for the invasion of Honshu. The Americans were expecting a bloody battle for the Japanese homeland, but unknown, except to a few, a compelling weapon was about to be introduced into warfare.

On August 7, President Truman shocked the world with the announcement of the first atom bomb drop on Hiroshima, which was followed by another on August 9 on Nagasaki. In Japan the news was devastating and spurred the government to bring an end to hostilities as soon as possible. On August 10, the Emperor directed a message through the Swiss government that Japan generally accepted the Potsdam ultimatum, with one exception. The Japanese response stated, "the declaration does not comprise any demand which prejudices the prerogatives of His Majesty as a Sovereign Ruler." The acceptance of "unconditional surrender" with this blatant exception was quickly rebuked by the United States in a reply on August 11, which stated, "From the moment of surrender the authority of the Emperor and the Japanese government to rule the state shall be subject to the Supreme Commander for Allied Powers who will take such steps as he deems proper to effectuate the surrender terms."

While the Japanese considered their next move, American offen-

6. Tokyo in ruins. The high-spirited attitude in Japan received a "wake up call" on April 19, 1942, when Col. James Doolittle launched the first bombing mission from the carrier "Hornet." Though barely within range of Japan, most of the B-25s managed to drop their bombs and fly to China. Some planes crashed in Japan, where crews were reportedly beheaded. Though physical damage of the bombing was limited, the psychological effect was great. As American forces came closer to Japan in 1944, massive conventional bomb and incendiary attacks wiped out large areas of major cities. About 200,000 civilian casualties were counted in the Tokyo area alone as hundreds of thousands of buildings and homes were destroyed by bombs or raging fires. Still the Japanese persisted in fighting and resisted acceptance of peace terms— until the horrors of atomic bombs were unleashed.

sive attacks were put on hold, though the build up for the invasion continued. For three days the lives of millions hung in the balance, then, on August 15, the United States received Japan's notification of surrender, to the relief of all. That same day President Truman announced that Gen. Douglas MacArthur was appointed Supreme Commander for the Allied Powers.

If the people believed what the government propagandists had been telling them, or if they knew of their own army's behavior as conquerors, they could only expect that the worse was yet to come. They were a nation of fearful people, afraid for their personal safety, afraid for what was left of their families, afraid that their government would be dissolved as they became captives of a foreign power, afraid that their industries would be totally destroyed, and afraid that the Emperor would be disgraced and removed, or even executed. Never before in the history of Japan had the country faced such an ominous future.

IV
THE MAKING
OF A
DEMOCRATIC NATION

Millions of words have been written about what led Japan into the war with the United States and who was responsible for Japan's transgressions. The central question regards the culpability of the Emperor (Hirohito) himself. No higher authority on the subject can be found than the Emperor as he answered in an unequivocal statement at the first meeting with General MacArthur at the American Embassy. He said, "For every political and military decision taken by my people in the conduct of the war I bear sole responsibility." Was this statement just a show of responsibility of a leader, or was it a sincere confession? This is known only in the heart of the Emperor.

What did the General really think of this statement? Clearly, he was relieved and pleased to hear it, but what did he truly understand? We cannot know the answer to that with certainty, either. Suffice to say that these two great leaders, at this critical stage of Japan's occupation, both embraced the concept that they needed each other for the success of their mutual mission.

Whatever a person has been in the past, whatever thoughts he held need not restrict what he does in the present and future. It matters little to subsequent events if the Emperor re-invented himself after the war; he should be judged *for that time* by his deeds, which were commendable. Clearly, he dedicated himself to restoring the well-being of the Japanese people and made great sacrifices and contributions to that end.

General MacArthur had a high regard for the Emperor, greatly respected his views, and most important, depended on him to carry the hearts and minds of the people toward democracy. Again, we cannot fathom the depth of the General's sincerity, but his treatment of the Emperor was beyond reproach. He was the pillar that stood between the Emperor and world leaders who were clamoring to have him tried as a war criminal. The General, however, never wavered in his support.

Nearly twenty years later, General MacArthur wrote his biography. Relying on notes, reports, and his own memory, he added the perspective of contemplative thought that the intervening period provided. He completed this work just before his death. His words, which are presented in the following pages go far beyond a recollection of things that happened. They give the reader a sense of the General's thought processes and his innermost convictions and emotions. By permission of the General MacArthur Foundation, we are reprinting the portion which covers the Japan Occupation period.

Note: The following passages are in the General's own words from his book, <u>Reminiscences</u>,[2] and will be set off by a vertical bar. Headings have been added for reference purposes, whereas none are given in the original text. Text within boxes has been added by the author or other writers for clarification or emphasis.

---

[2] Douglas A. MacArthur, <u>Reminiscences</u>, McGraw-Hill Book Company, New York, 1964

Surrender

The formal ceremonies of surrender aboard the Missouri were fixed for September 2, 1945. I had received no instructions as to what to say or what to do. I was on my own, standing on the quarterdeck with only God and my own conscience to guide me.

I have read several accounts of what occurred and what was said that morning, but my favorite of all is that which was officially rendered to the Emperor after it was over by a Japanese member of the surrender party, Mr. Toshikazu Kase, an alumnus of Amherst and Harvard, and a Japanese diplomat of twenty years service with the foreign office.

Kase's report follows

It was a surprisingly cool day for early September. The sky was dull gray with clouds hanging low. We left Tokyo at about five o'clock in the morning. There were nine of us, three each from the Foreign Office, and the War and Navy Departments, besides the two delegates, Shigemitsu, the Foreign Minister representing the government, and General Umezu, the Chief of Staff of the Army representing the Supreme Command. With the two delegates leading the procession, our cars sped at full speed on the battered and bumpy road to Yokohama. Along the highway, we could see nothing but miles and miles of debris and destruction where there had once flourished towns containing a great number of munitions factories. The ghastly sight of death and desolation was enough to freeze my heart. These hollow ruins, however, were perhaps a fit prelude to the poignant drama in which we were about to take part, for were we not sorrowing men come to seek a tomb for a fallen Empire? They were also a grim reminder that a nation was snatched from an impending annihilation. For were not the scenes of havoc the atomic bomb wrought a sufficient warning? The waste of war and the ignominy of surrender were put on my mental loom and pro-

7. Japanese surrender - September 2, 1945. The delegation of Japanese was headed by diplomat Shigemitsu (seated, insert) and Chief of the Imperial General Staff, General Umezu (not shown). All Allied commanders and staff were present, along with hundreds of reporters, cameramen, ship's officers and crew for this historic signing. In a remarkable display of consideration, General MacArthur asked two of his military commanders to stand by him during the signing, Gen. Wainwright (U.S.) and Gen. Percival (U.K.) This was not to recognize their great battle victories, but to honor them for their gallantry in defeat, when they were forced to surrender to overwhelming Japanese forces at Corregidor and Singapore. *(U.S. Army Photo)*

duced a strange fabric of grief and sorrow. There were few men on the road and none probably recognized us. Our journey was kept in utmost secrecy in order to avoid publicity lest extremists might attempt to impede us by violence.

To begin with, there was much ado in selecting the delegates. Nobody wanted to volunteer for the odious duty. The Prime Minister, Prince Higashikuni, was the Emperor's uncle and was considered unsuitable on that account. Next choice fell on Prince Konoye, who was Vice Premier and the real power in the government, but he shunned the ordeal. Finally the mission was assigned to Shigemitsu, the Foreign Minister. On accepting the imperial command to sign the surrender document as principal delegate, he confided to me what an honor he felt it, since it was the mark of the Sovereign's confidence in him. Shigemitsu served twice before as Foreign Minister — namely, in the latter period of the Tojo Cabinet and through the duration of the succeeding Koiso Cabinet. He is a man of confirmed peaceful views and during his twelve months' term of office did his utmost to prepare for an early termination of the war. His efforts, in which I assisted him to the best of my ability, were in fact powerfully instrumental in expediting the restoration of peace. Such being the case, there was reason to believe that unlike others who evaded the mission, hating it as unbearably onerous, Shigemitsu regarded it as a painful but profitable task. In his mind he was determined to make this day of national mortification the starting point for a renewed pilgrimage onward toward the goal, though dim and distant, of a peaceful state. If this day marked a journey's end it must also signify a journey's beginning. Only the traveler to grief must be replaced by the traveler to glory.

Not so with General Umezu, who reluctantly accepted the appointment as the second delegate. He had opposed the termination of hostilities to the last moment and was, more-

INSTRUMENT OF SURRENDER

We, acting by command of and in behalf of the Emperor of Japan, the Japanese Government and the Japanese Imperial General Headquarters, hereby accept the provisions set forth in the declaration issued by the heads of the Governments of the United States, China and Great Britain on 26 July 1945, at Potsdam, and subsequently adhered to by the Union of Soviet Socialist Republics, which four powers are hereafter referred to as the Allied Powers.

We hereby proclaim the unconditional surrender to the Allied Powers of the Japanese Imperial General Headquarters and of all Japanese armed forces and all armed forces under Japanese control wherever situated.

We hereby command all Japanese forces wherever situated and the Japanese people to cease hostilities forthwith, to preserve and save from damage all ships, aircraft, and military and civil property and to comply with all requirements which may be imposed by the Supreme Commander for the Allied Powers or by agencies of the Japanese Government at his direction.

We hereby command the Japanese Imperial General Headquarters to issue at once orders to the Commanders of all Japanese forces and all forces under Japanese control wherever situated to surrender unconditionally themselves and all forces under their control.

We hereby command all civil, military and naval officials to obey and enforce all proclamations, orders and directives deemed by the Supreme Commander for the Allied Powers to be proper to effectuate this surrender and issued by him or under his authority and we direct all such officials to remain at their posts and to continue to perform their non-combatant duties unless specifically relieved by him or under his authority.

We hereby undertake for the Emperor, the Japanese Government and their successors to carry out the provisions of the Potsdam Declaration in good faith, and to issue whatever orders and take whatever action may be required by the Supreme Commander for the Allied Powers or by any other designated representative of the Allied Powers for the purpose of giving effect to that Declaration.

We hereby command the Japanese Imperial Government and the Japanese Imperial General Headquarters at once to liberate all allied prisoners of war and civilian internees now under Japanese control and to provide for their protection, care, maintenance and immediate transportation to places as directed.

The authority of the Emperor and the Japanese Government to rule the state shall be subject to the Supreme Commander for the Allied Powers who will take such steps as he deems proper to effectuate these terms of surrender.

8. Instrument of surrender. This remarkable document was written on a single page in concise and definitive terms. The document is a model of brevity. In today's verbose world, it would probably fill books.

9. Instrument of surrender. The instrument was signed by Shigemitsu for the Emperor and by Gen. Umezu for the Imperial General Headquarters. Allied representatives signing were from the United States, China, United Kingdom, USSR, Australia, Canada, France, Netherlands, and New Zealand.

over, a soldier born to command and not to sue. When he was recommended for the mission he grew, so it is reported, pale with anger and laconically remarked that if it was forced upon him, he would instantly commit hara-kiri in protest. It required the Emperor's personal persuasion to make him execute the duties with good grace.

It may sound somewhat silly, but as precautions were then deemed necessary, the appointment of two delegates was not intimated to the press until the last moment. The names of nine persons who accompanied them were not published at all as the service officers were against this, though these names had been communicated to and approved by the Allied authorities. Such, indeed, was the temper of the times.

This party arrived in Yokohama in less than an hour's time. It was on this day that the spearhead of the U.S. Eighth Army landed at the same port. Sentries with gleaming bayonets were heavily guarding the streets through which we rode slowly to the port area. All the cars had removed the flags on the bonnet and officers had left their swords behind at the office of the Prefectural Governor where we rested a while. We had thus furled the banner and ungirt the sword. Diplomats without flag and soldiers without sword — sullen and silent we continued the journey till we reached the quay.

There were four destroyers with white placards hung on the mast marked A to D. We boarded the one marked B, which was the Lansdown, a ship which saw much meritorious service in the battle of the Pacific. As the destroyer pushed out of the harbor, we saw in the offing lines on lines of gray warships, both heavy and light, anchored in majestic array. This was the mighty pageant of the Allied navies that so lately belched forth their crashing battle, now holding in their swift thunder and floating like calm sea birds on the subjugated waters. A spirit of gay festivity pervaded the atmosphere.

After about an hour's cruise the destroyer stopped in full view of the battleship Missouri, which lay anchored some eighteen miles off the shore. The huge 45,000 tonner towered high above the rest of the proud squadron. High on the mast there fluttered in the wind the Stars and Stripes. It was this flag that has lighted the marching step of America's destiny on to shining victory. Today this flag of glory was raised in triumph to mark the Big Day. As we approached the battle-ship in a motor launch, our eyes were caught by rows of sailors massed on her broadside lining the rails, a starry mul-titude, in their glittering uniforms of immaculate white.

Soon the launch came alongside the battleship, and we climbed its gangway, Shigemitsu leading the way, heavily limping on his cane. For he walks on a wooden leg, having had his leg blown off by a bomb outrage in Shanghai some fifteen years ago. It was as if he negotiated each step with a groan and we, the rest of us, echoed it with a sigh. As we, eleven in all, climbed onto the veranda deck on the starboard side, we gathered into three short rows facing the representa-tives of the Allied powers across a table covered with green cloth, on which were placed the white documents of surren-der. The veranda deck was animated by a motley of sparkling colors, red, gold, brown, and olive, as decorations and ribbons decked the uniforms of different cut and color worn by the Allied representatives. There were also row upon row of American admirals and generals in somber khaki; but what added to the festive gaiety of the occasion was the sight of the war correspondents who, monkey-like, hung on to every cliff-like point of vantage in most precarious postures. Evidently scaffolding had been specially constructed for the conve-nience of the cameramen, who were working frantically on their exciting job. Then there was a gallery of spectators who seemed numberless, overcrowding every bit of available space on the great ship, on the mast, on the chimneys, on the gun turrets — on everything and everywhere.

They were all thronged, packed to suffocation, representatives, journalists, spectators, an assembly of brass, braid, and brand. As we appeared on the scene we were, I felt, being subjected to the torture of the pillory. There were a million eyes beating us in the million shafts of a rattling storm of arrows barbed with fire. I felt their keenness sink into my body with a sharp physical pain. Never have I realized that the glance of glaring eyes could hurt so much.

We waited for a few minutes standing in the public gaze like penitent boys awaiting the dreaded schoolmaster. I tried to preserve with the utmost sangfroid the dignity of defeat, but it was difficult and every minute seemed to contain ages. I looked up and saw painted on the wall nearby several miniature Rising Suns, our flag, evidently in numbers corresponding to the planes and submarines shot down or sunk by the crew of the battleship. As I tried to count these markings, tears rose in my throat and quickly gathered to the eyes, flooding them. I could hardly bear the sight now. Heroes of unwritten stories, they were young boys who defied death gaily and gallantly, manning the daily thinning ranks of the suicide corps. They were just like cherry blossoms, emblems of our national character, all of a sudden blooming into riotous beauty and just as quickly going away. What do they see today, their spirit, the glorious thing, looking down on the scene of our surrender?

MacArthur walks quietly from the interior of the ship and steps to the microphones:

"We are gathered here, representatives of the major warring powers," he said, *"to conclude a solemn agreement whereby peace may be restored. The issues, involving divergent ideals and ideologies, have been determined on the bat-*

tlefields of the world and hence are not fo
debate. Nor is it for us here to meet, repres
majority of the people of the earth, in a spirit
ice or hatred. But rather it is for us, both vi
quished, to rise to that higher dignity which al
sacred purposes we are about to serve, commit
people unreservedly to faithful compliance with
tion they are here formally to assume.

"It is my earnest hope and indeed the hope
mankind that from this solemn occasion a better world
emerge out of the blood and carnage of the past — a w
founded upon faith and understanding — a world dedica.
to the dignity of man and the fulfillment of his most cherishe
wish — for freedom, tolerance and justice.

"The terms and conditions upon which the surrender of
the Japanese Imperial Forces is here to be given and accept-
ed are contained in the instrument of surrender now before
you.

"As Supreme Commander for the Allied Powers, I
announce it my firm purpose, in the tradition of the countries
I represent, to proceed in the discharge of my responsibilities
with justice and tolerance, while taking all necessary dispo-
sitions to insure that the terms of surrender are fully, prompt-
ly and faithfully complied with."

In a few minutes' time the speech was over and the
Supreme Commander invited the Japanese delegates to sign
the instrument of surrender. Shigemitsu signed first followed
by Umedzu. It was eight minutes past nine when MacArthur
put his signature to the documents. Other representatives of
the Allied Powers followed suit in the order of the United
States, China, the United Kingdom, the Soviet Union,
Australia, Canada, France, the Netherlands and New Zealand.

10. Gen. MacArthur on Japanese homeland, August 30, 1945. General Douglas MacArthur, Supreme Commander Allied Powers, flanked by staff officers and press, makes his way across the Atsugi airfield to an ancient Lincoln sedan, provided by the Japanese, which would take him to temporary quarters in the New Grand Hotel in Yokohama. Japan was not a new experience for the General. He had visited on friendly terms in 1905 as an aide to his father Gen. Arthur MacArthur, who was on a diplomatic/military tour following the cessation of the Russo-Japanese War. *(U.S. Army Photo)*

When all the representatives had finished signing, MacArthur announced slowly:

"Let us pray that peace be now restored to the world and that God will preserve it always. These proceedings are closed."

At that moment, the skies parted and the sun shone brightly through the layers of clouds. There was a steady drone above and now it became a deafening roar and an armada of airplanes paraded into sight, sweeping over the warships. Four hundred B-29 bombers and 1500 carrier planes joined in the aerial pageant in a final salute. It was over.

MacArthur later broadcast to the American people from Japan:

"Today the guns are silent. A great tragedy has ended. A great victory has been won. The skies no longer rain death — the seas bear only commerce — men everywhere walk upright in the sunlight. The entire world is quietly at peace. The holy mission has been completed. And in reporting this to you, the people, I speak for the thousands of silent lips, forever stilled among the jungles and the beaches and in the deep waters of the Pacific which marked the way. I speak for the unnamed brave millions homeward bound to take up the challenge of that future which they did so much to salvage from the brink of disaster.

"As I look back on the long, tortuous trail from those grim days of Bataan and Corregidor, when an entire world lived in fear, when democracy was on the defensive everywhere, when modern civilization trembled in the balance, I thank a merciful God that He has given us the faith, the courage and the power from which to mold victory. We have known the bitterness of defeat and the exultation of triumph, and from both we have learned there can be no turning back. We must go forward to preserve in peace what we won in war.

"A new era is upon us. Even the lesson of victory itself brings with it profound concern, both for our future security and the survival of civilization. The destructiveness of the war potential, through progressive advances in scientific discovery, has in fact now reached a point which revises the traditional concept of war.

"Men since the beginning of time have sought peace. Various methods through the ages have attempted to devise an international process to prevent or settle disputes between nations. From the very start workable methods were found insofar as individual citizens were concerned, but the mechanics of an instrumentality of larger international scope have never been successful. Military alliances, balances of power, leagues of nations, all in turn failed, leaving the only path to be by way of the crucible of war. We have had our last chance. If we do not now devise some greater and more equitable system, Armageddon will be at our door. The problem basically is theological and involves a spiritual recrudescence and improvement of human character that will synchronize with our almost matchless advances in science, art, literature and all material and cultural developments of the past two thousand years. It must be of the spirit if we are to save the flesh.

"We stand in Tokyo today reminiscent of our countryman, Commodore Perry, ninety-two years ago. His purpose was to bring to Japan an era of enlightenment and progress, by lifting the veil of isolation to the friendship, trade, and commerce of the world. But alas, the knowledge thereby gained of Western science was forged into an instrument of oppression and human enslavement. Freedom of expression, freedom of action, even freedom of thought were denied through appeal to superstition, and through the application of force. We are committed by the Potsdam Declaration of Principles to see that the Japanese people are liberated from this condition of slavery. It is my purpose to implement this commitment just

as rapidly as the armed forces are demobilized and other essential steps taken to neutralize the war potential.

"The energy of the Japanese race, if properly directed, will enable expansion vertically rather than horizontally. If the talents of the race are turned into constructive channels, the country can lift itself from its present deplorable state into a position of dignity.

"To the Pacific basin has come the vista of a new emancipated world. Today, freedom is on the offensive, democracy is on the march. Today, in Asia as well as in Europe, unshackled peoples are tasting the full sweetness of liberty, the relief from fear.

"Add so, my fellow countrymen, today I report to you that your sons and daughters have served you well and faithfully with the calm, deliberate, determined fighting spirit of the American soldier and sailor, based upon a tradition of historical truth as against the fanaticism of an enemy supported only by mythological fiction. Their spiritual strength and power has brought us through to victory. They are homeward bound — take care of them."

When the Supreme Commander finished, I wrote in my report the impression his words had made on me. He is a man of peace. Never has the truth of the line "peace has her victories no less renowned than war" been more eloquently demonstrated. He is a man of light. Radiantly, the gathering rays of his magnanimous soul embrace the earth, his footsteps paving the world with light. Is it not a piece of rare good fortune, I asked myself, that a man of such caliber and character should have been designated as the Supreme Commander who will shape the destiny of Japan? In the dark hour of our despair and distress, a bright light is ushered in, in the very person of General MacArthur. While the destroyer sped home, I wrote down hurriedly the impressions of the surrender ceremony which Shigemitsu took to the Throne immediately after our return to the Capital, as the Emperor was anxiously waiting for his report. At the end of this report in which I dwelt at length upon the superb address of the Supreme Commander, I raised a question whether it would have been possible for us, had we been victorious, to embrace the vanquished with a similar magnanimity. Clearly it would have been different. Returning from the audience, Shigemitsu told me that the Emperor nodded with a sigh in agreement. Indeed, a distance inexpressible by numbers separates us — America from Japan. After all, we were not beaten on the battlefield by dint of superior arms, we were defeated in the spiritual contest by virtue of a nobler idea. The real issue was moral — beyond all the powers of algebra to compute.

The day will come when recorded time, age on age, will seem but a point in retrospect. However, happen what may in the future, this Big Day on the Missouri will stand out as one of the brightest dates in history, with General MacArthur as a shining obelisk in the desert of human endeavor that marks a timeless march onward toward an enduring peace.

Conclusion of Kase's report

Some deep reflections by the General

This most favorable impression of a Japanese diplomat differed completely with everything that the Japanese government had been telling its people for years. The philosophy I had expressed, based upon the truth that men may be destroyed by what they have and what they know, but that they may be saved by what they are, produced a most favorable result, immediate and unqualified. Just as I understood them, so they reacted with irresistible energy in the creation of a new Japan.

Trying to recall my emotions and impressions as I prepared to receive the surrender of the mighty warlords of the Far East, I wish that my pen were wielded by one on such intimate terms with words — those immortal heralds of thought which at the touch of genius become radiant — that at my call they would convey my feelings in terms that would satisfy the ultimate sources of reason, history, and interpretation. For I have a consciousness that in the events culminating at this immortal moment lie those truths which at last are transplanted into epics and lyrics, and those exalted terms which we find on the lips of the great seers and prophets.

Was the day beclouded by mists and trailing clouds? Were there lone trees cresting Tokyo's shores against the moving sky? Were there voices of waters falling far up within some wild ravine racing into the bay? Were there nearby fields where bees were buzzing? I cannot remember, but this I do — the all-embracing pride I felt in my country's monumental victory. Its future seemed to gleam as though seen through the optimistic gates of youth.

I told myself, the tide of world affairs may ebb and flow, old empires may die, new nations be born; alliances may arise, thrive, wither and vanish — but in its effort to build economic growth and prosperity, an atmosphere of hope and freedom, a community of strength and unity of purpose, a lasting peace of justice, my own beloved country now leads the world. It points the way to an age of evolution, in which the brain of man will abstract from the universe its fundamental secrets. Today's wonders will become tomorrow's obsolescence. We stand on the threshold of a new life. What vast panoramas will open before us none can say. They are there, just beyond the horizon, just over there. And they are of a magnificence and a diversity far beyond the comprehension of anyone here today. This new world would have no boundaries — no lost horizons. Its limits would be as broad as the spirit and the imagination of man.

But with this exaltation of pride, my soul saddened as my thoughts turned to my faithful men-at-arms. I had seen them die at Verdun,

11. American troops enter Japan. Elements of the 1st Calvary Division are seen marching into Tokyo. This division, famous from frontier days and the Civil War, fought with distinction in the Pacific Theater. Less than five years later, they would leave Japan for another war in Korea. *(U.S. Army Photo)*

at St. Mihiel, at Guadalcanal; in the foxholes of Bataan and the, batteries of Corregidor; on land, on sea, and in the air; amidst swamp and jungle, hot sands, and frozen reaches; in the knee-deep mud of shell-shocked roads and dripping trenches. They were the driving soul of Americanism. They had given me an abiding faith in the future of this nation — a faith based on the invincible character of the American people. A faith that once again they had restored to our beloved country the serenity of hope without fear. A faith in the course of our destiny as a free, prosperous, and happy people.

And, from the other side...

Eleven months later I received from then Prime Minister Shigeru Yoshida the following missive revealing the sentiments of the ruling classes regarding the surrender and its immediate aftermath.

Dear General:

This morning I noticed in one of our newspapers, the *Mainichi Shimbun,* August 15, a story of Japan's surrender as told by Baron Kantaro Suzuki, then our Prime Minister.

What he says at the end of the narrative has my unqualified endorsement. His attitude and sentiments at the time of the momentous decision were not only the attitude and sentiments of His Majesty but also, I am quite sure, of the vast majority of the inarticulate but right-minded men in the street throughout Japan. I enclose an English translation of the particular portion of the article signed by Admiral Suzuki himself. Yours sincerely, Shigeru Yoshida

The enclosure read as follows:

"Calm and serene was my feeling at the time of making the surrender. People about me were much worried. Some insisted that we should negotiate to get a definite guarantee from the Allies regarding the preservation of our national structure. But such a proposition seemed essentially illogical, and I did not care to go to the trouble of taking it up. My position was this: we were defeated, and as long as we admitted our defeat, the only manly thing to do was to leave everything to the victor. Such had been the military tradition from ancient times. Only I had one absolute conviction as to what to do. That was to trust the enemy commander.

"The 'Bushido' is not a Japanese monopoly. It is an universal code. To protect your adversary who has surrendered as one enlisted on your side is the way of the warrior. I did not know about the personality of General MacArthur, but I myself as a soldier had a firm trust in this soldierly spirit. Therefore, despite all manner of disquieting rumors born of fear and uncertainty in those days I had not the least apprehension. In this respect His Majesty felt exactly the same as I did. As is well known, His Majesty never inclined to suspect others. He even commanded me to confide in the enemy and to place everything at his disposal.

"The last audience I had was in the middle of June 1946, when I resigned from the presidency of the Privy Council. On that occasion His Majesty said to me that the occupation policy of Supreme Commander MacArthur was fair and just, and things were progressing quite satisfactorily. Now with the full realization that I was right in my conviction about trusting in the enemy commander.

"I am watching from my country place of retirement the operation of the Allied occupation policy and the progress of the democratization of Japan. I am very happy to know that the course on which I chose to steer the nation to the termination of war has proved by no means a bad thing for Japan."

Kantaro Suzuki

12. Gaijin Shogun - Gen. Douglas MacArthur. The calamitous defeat and surrender of Japan ending WWII was followed by occupation with foreign troops for the first time in Japan's history. Gen. Douglas MacArthur, as Supreme Commander Allied Powers, ruled Japan from September 30, 1945, until April 16, 1951. At an age when most men retired, the great American general, hero of two world wars, took on the daunting task of making a democratic nation from the remnants of a country devastated by war and disheartened by defeat. *(Photo by Johnny Florea)*

Japanese War Veterans

When they went off to war, they were regaled with celebrations and honors; when they returned, they were forgotten, slighted, ignored, or disabused. The veteran of a failed war is no hero, just a reminder of awful things past which seem better forgotten. Some civilians behave as if the veteran was at fault for the war, rather than being another victim.

When Americans returned from WWII, they were heroes, from the Korean War there were mixed reactions, from the Vietnam War, another failed war, the reception was probably like that which returning Japanese veterans experienced.

It borders on a national sin for a country to treat veterans poorly because it is far from what they deserve. Even if they are veterans from a failed or unpopular war, they should be treated with respect and kindness. The veterans neither initiated or promulgated the conflict; they behaved as dutiful citizens, supporting their country's agenda and risked their lives, limbs and spirits in the bargain. All returned wounded psychologically, if not bodily as well. They deserved praise for serving their country, regardles of the cause, and were at least entitled to the opportunity to heal physically and emotionally.

I find it telling that of the thousands of Japanese men I have met in the past fifty years, though many are of the proper age, none ever spoke of their war experiences. Even those I knew well enough to ask had little or nothing to say.

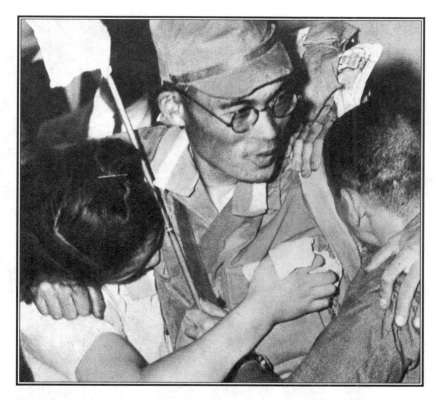

13. Japanese veteran returns to family reunion. For some there was joy and solace in returning to their families, but in every case it brought a new set of demands: support of the family, not just individual survival. These returning veterans saw nothing of the honors they enjoyed before leaving home. Understandably, all people had problems of their own but, unfortunately, the veterans also suffered lack of consideration which persisted even after the country recovered.

14. Japanese veterans and unhappy homecomings. After years of great personal sacrifice fighting in an ill-conceived war, the survivors are repatriated. For years, the thought of family was their only link to sanity and purpose. What a terrible shock for many to find that their homes were destroyed and that family members were dead or scattered, who knew where? A public sentiment of disdain, added to the above sorrow, created a veteran in great psychological despair and suffering.

Another experience which drew my attention to the Japanese veteran occurred at the Yasukuni Shrine, where I had gone one Spring weekend to view the cherry blossoms. There were a dozen or more Japanese men in rag-tag remnants of uniforms. Also, notable in contrast, were many brightly attired geisha in traditional dress, who seemed strangely supportive of the old soldiers. Later, when they gave forth in song, there were many tears. I asked my Japanese friend about their song. It was Dohi-no-sakura, the words tell "when the cherry blossoms fall, I'll remember you at Iwakuni," a tribute to lost comrades. I could feel their sorrow.

The reluctance or inability to freely demonstrate or speak of wartime experiences is a consequence of the public's attitude about the war. The prevailing wisdom seems to be, "If we don't talk about it, it's as if it never happened." There is another bit of wisdom that says, "If you don't learn from mistakes, you are doomed to repeat them."

This sentiment of silence may also have affected the government's attitude in determining what historical information is taught in schools. It is well-known that coverage of WWII and the Occupation is very limited in the Japanese educational curricula.

All veterans share in the pathos of war. At times remembering is painful, but it is good for the psyche, and probably the soul, to express this sorrow. It is unfortunate that veterans in Japan do not have a public Veterans Day, as we do in the U.S., when they can be open about who they are and join in with other veterans to vent their heavy hearts.

Naysayers
at home and abroad

But the approval of the masses of the people was in sharp contrast to the chilly reaction at the State Department in Washington and in the chancelleries of some of our European Allies. In an interview with United States Senator Claude Pepper of Florida, Generalissimo Joseph Stalin expressed apprehension that our occupation of Japan may be too "soft," and Foreign Commissar Molotov used the same argument in London when he demanded that I be replaced by a four-power commission. A magnanimous approach was far indeed from preconceived plans born in hate and dedicated to vengeance. The Soviets had already divined that, though I had defeated the Japanese in battle, I intended, by means of the concepts of a free world, to win them in peace.

There was a vehement press and radio campaign within the United States against retention of the Emperor. By and large, the same media and commentators who had been loudest in demanding that German industrial potential be destroyed, were now insisting that Hirohito and his family, and the complete Japanese government, be stamped out. Not unexpectedly, the Communist Daily Worker spearheaded this propaganda drive; several normally responsible New York papers took the same line, and a number of news analysts with national radio audiences echoed the assaults. Those who shouted for a merciless peace had no hesitation in slandering me as the supreme commander when they felt such a tactic would further their ends.

The Occupation begins

As contingents of the Eighth Army proceeded to unload in Tokyo Bay on September 4th, an extraordinary meeting of the Diet was summoned to hear the Emperor's speech and Prime Minister Higashi-Kuni's summary of the factors that had culminated in the imperial decision to capitulate. For the first time in history the Emperor addressed his people personally, ordering them to submit to the terms of surrender and to strive to re-establish a position of trust and respect in the world. He explained that he had followed the path of submission to improve Japan's precarious position, underlining the need for self-discipline and composure. For his subjects this meant a directive to work in peace, and marked a new phase in the history of Japan.

I did not visit Tokyo for the first time until six days after the surrender ceremonies. It was just 22 miles from the New Grand Hotel in Yokohama to the American Embassy, which was to be my home throughout the Occupation, but they were 22 miles of devastation and vast piles of charred rubble.

I established headquarters in the Dai Ichi Building in downtown Tokyo, across from the moat surrounding the Emperor's palace. The pattern of government was unique in modern annals. I, a professional soldier, had the civil responsibility and absolute control over almost 80 million people, and I would maintain that control until Japan had once more demonstrated that it was ready, willing, and able to become a responsible member of the family of free nations. Never in history had a nation and its people been more completely crushed than were the Japanese at the end of the war. They had suffered more than a military debacle, more than the destruction of their armed forces, more than the elimination of their industrial bases, more even than the occupation of their land by foreign bayonets. Their entire faith in the Japanese way of life, cherished as invincible for many centuries, perished in the agony of their total defeat. The impact of such a disaster was probably greater than had ever been experienced in modern history. The extraordinary feudalism which had prevailed in this isolated land had resulted in almost mythological and fanatical belief in the invincibility of its arms and the superiority of its culture.

The old policies

Although lacking in iron, coal, metals, cotton, oil, and nearly all commodity essentials, Japan had prospered in the past century largely because of the thrift and industry of its people. By trade and barter it imported raw materials — the wool of Australia, the cotton of America, the rubber and tin and oil of Malaya and the East Indies — and with its cheap labor and transportation supplied the markets of the millions of the coolie class throughout Asia who could not afford the more costly manufactured goods of Europe and America.

Its basic policy and purpose over the years had been to secure the bases which supplied its manufacturing plants. It had absorbed Formosa, Korea, and Manchuria, and was attempting to bring China under its control. It had prospered and poured billions of its profits into these outlying areas. Indeed, one of the contributing causes of the war had been its fear of the economic sanctions of the Allies initiated by President Roosevelt. Rightly or wrongly, it felt that this course would paralyze its industry and lead to internal revolution. It had hoped to seize and hold the bases contributing to its industrial empire and thus ensure for all time its so-called "Greater East Asia Co-Prosperity Sphere."

All during the war its people had been deluded into believing they were winning. Now, in one dreadful moment, all this was to change. Ruin and disaster never conceived possible had engulfed them. In their hour of agony, like all human beings, they turned to their religious faiths to bolster them. But even these failed them at the crucial moment. Shintoism and Buddhism had become so absorbed by governmental control as to be almost an integral part of the fascist hierarchy of leadership.

Personal challenge

Because I had been given so much power, I was faced with the most difficult situation of my life. Power is one thing. The problem of how to administer it is another. My professional military knowledge was no longer sufficient. I needed the skills of a manufacturing executive, a teacher, even a theologian of sorts. I had to rebuild a nation that had been almost completely destroyed by the war.

Whatever my ethical teachings had been, whatever my basic character was, whatever the concept of mankind that lay within my soul, I would have to bring into this political, economic, and spiritual vacuum concepts of honor, justice, and compassion. Japan had become the world's great laboratory for an experiment in the liberation of a people from totalitarian military rule and for the liberalization of government from within. It was clear that the experiment in Japan must go far beyond the primary purpose of the Allies — the destruction of Japan's ability to wage another war and the punishment of war criminals. Yet history clearly showed that no modern military occupation of a conquered nation had been a success.

Past failures

Military occupation was not new to me. I had garrisoned on the west bank of the Rhine as commander of the Rainbow Division at

45

the end of World War 1. At first hand, I had seen what I thought were basic and fundamental weaknesses in prior forms of military occupations: the substitution of civil by military authority; the loss of self-respect and self-confidence by the people; the constantly growing ascendency of centralized dictatorial power instead of a localized and representative system; the lowering of the spiritual and moral tone of a population controlled by foreign bayonets; the inevitable deterioration in the occupying forces themselves as the disease of power infiltrated their ranks and bred a sort of race superiority. If any occupation lasts too long, or is not carefully watched from the start, one party becomes slaves and the other masters. History teaches, too, that almost every military occupation breeds new wars of the future. I had studied the lives of Alexander and Caesar and Napoleon, and great as these captains were, all had erred when they became the leaders of occupation forces. I tried to remember the lessons my own father had taught me, lessons learned out of his experiences as military governor of the Philippines, but I was assailed by the gravest misgivings. With such hazards as I anticipated, could I succeed? My doubts were to be my best safeguard, my fears my greatest strength.

From the moment of my appointment as supreme commander, I had formulated the policies I intended to follow, implementing them through the Emperor and the machinery of the imperial government. I was thoroughly familiar with Japanese administration, its weaknesses and its strengths, and felt the reforms I contemplated were those which would bring Japan abreast of modern progressive thought and action. First destroy the military power. Punish war criminals. Build the structure of representative government. Modernize the constitution. Hold free elections. Enfranchise the women. Release the political prisoners. Liberate the farmers. Establish a free labor movement. Encourage a free economy. Abolish police oppression. Develop a free and responsible press. Liberalize education. Decentralize the political power. Separate church from state.

These tasks were to occupy me for the next five years and more. All were eventually accomplished, some easily, some with difficulty. But as the reforms progressed and freedom increasingly came to the Japanese masses, a unique bond of mutual faith developed between the Japanese people and the supreme commander. As they increasingly sensed my insistence upon just treatment for them, even at times against the great nations I represented, they came to regard me not as a conqueror, but as a protector. I had a deep responsibility as guardian of these people so dramatically brought under my charge. I felt they needed spiritual leadership as well as material administration. I cautioned our troops from the start that by their conduct our own country would be judged in world opinion, that success or failure of the occupation could well rest upon their poise and self-restraint. Their general conduct was beyond criticism. Many ancient customs of the Japanese, bred by isolation, gave way before the example they set, and admiration for them was aroused in Japanese hearts. They were truly ambassadors of good will.

Letting the Japanese find a new cultural path

I carefully abstained from any interferences by edict with the cultural traditions or the personal Japanese way of life. In frequent public statements I advised the Japanese people to seek a healthy blend between the best of theirs and the best of ours, and I was careful to tell them that no people or country was sufficient unto itself in these matters. I encouraged delegations of Japanese from every walk of life to travel in the West, and where it was possible,

I paved the way for such visits. I have always felt that one of the things that made the occupation a success was my insistence that we wanted to learn from the Japanese as well as teach them. It had a great deal to do with restoring a sense of dignity and purpose in their people, and as they regained self-respect and pride, they approached an exchange of ideas with avidity and good will. This mutual respect became the foundation of the basic esteem our two peoples came to have for one another — and enabled the occupation to write a unique and warmly human chapter of world history.

Shackles of centuries

The extent of some of our problems went far beyond anything that we could possibly have imagined at the moment of the cease-fire in the summer of 1945. Supposedly, the Japanese were a twentieth-century civilization. In reality, they were more nearly a feudal society, of the type discarded by Western nations some four centuries ago. There were aspects of Japanese life that went even farther back than that. Although theocracy was a system of government that had been thoroughly discredited by 3000 years of progress in the Western world, it still existed in Japan. The Emperor was considered a divine being, and the average Japanese subject dared not even lift up his eyes to view his ruler. This God-Emperor was absolute. His word was final. He was bolstered in power by a small group of families who controlled the military, the apparatus of government, and the economy. There was no such thing as civil rights. There were not even human rights. The property and produce of the average Japanese individual could be taken away from him in whole or in part as it suited the ruling cliques. Between 1937 and 1940 more than 60,000 people were thrown into prison for "dangerous thinking" by the secret police. Indeed, an American viewing Japan would be inclined to class it as more nearly akin to ancient Sparta than to any modern nation.

Fear of reprisals and abuse

Let there be no mistake about the extent of Japan's defeat in the war. It was completely crushed. Part of the defeat was physical, with factories, homes, and whole cities destroyed. But another part of that defeat was spiritual. For almost four years the Japanese people had expected nothing but victory. Every bulletin blared of success. Not only that, the people had been told they were fighting a kind of holy crusade against barbarians who had no respect for anything. The war must be won to prevent rape, murder, and other unspeakable crimes. As a leader of the American forces, the Japanese government concentrated on me. When American troops landed in Japan in August 1945, the image of the sadistic commander and his rapacious soldiery was in every Japanese mind.

From the very beginning I tried to erase this false conception. In my speech aboard the Missouri I had very carefully tried to reassure the Japanese people, and a few days later, when I moved my headquarters into the Dai Ichi Building, I made a public statement that "SCAP is not concerned with how to keep Japan down, but how to get her on her feet again." I underlined again and again that we had several missions. It was true that we intended to destroy Japan as a militarist power. It was true that we intended to impose penalties for past wrongs. These things had been set out in the surrender terms. But we also felt that we could best accomplish our purpose by building a new kind of Japan, one that would give the Japanese people freedom and justice, and some kind of security. I was determined that our principles during the occupation would be the same principles for which our soldiers had fought on the battlefield.

15. Mass starvation dominates priorities. The food shortage was so intense after the war that streets were torn up so that crops could be planted, as shown here in the shadow of the National Diet. Gen. MacArthur immediately turned massive stores of military rations over to the Japanese and arranged for the start of worldwide efforts to bring emergency supplies to the starving Japanese.

Fear of mass starvation

So effective had been the blockade established by our air and sea forces during the war that the Japanese food supplies had become insufficient for the civil population. Starvation threatened many communities which had been severely bombed. Under Japanese armies of occupation, conquered populations, despite their poverty, had been expected to provide not only full, but even luxurious provisions for the invaders. The Japanese had no reason to expect anything other when the situation was reversed. But as soon as the complete exhaustion of Japanese food resources was confirmed, I issued an order forbidding the consumption by the occupation forces of local food and requested Washington to begin at once shipment of relief supplies. The effect was instantaneous. The Japanese authorities changed their attitude from one of correct politeness to one of open trust. The press, which had been dubious at first, now began to voice unanimous praise.

Russians try to partition Japan

The Russians commenced to make trouble from the very beginning. They demanded that their troops should occupy Hokkaido, the northern island of Japan, and thus divide the country in two. Their forces were not to be under the control of the supreme commander, but entirely independent of his authority. I refused point blank. General Derevyanko, became almost abusive and threatened that the Soviet Union would see to it that I would be dismissed as supreme commander. He went so far as to say Russian forces would move in whether I approved or not. I told him that if a single Soviet soldier entered Japan without my authority, I would at once throw the entire Russian Mission, including himself, into jail. He listened and stared as though he could not believe his own ears, and then said politely enough, "By God, I

16. Japanese cyclotrons destroyed. This ranks high on the list of blunders made by Americans. Bureaucrats in the War Department overruled Gen. MacArthur's recommendation to preserve the cyclotrons for scientific purposes, and ordered their destruction. Dr. Karl T. Compton, president of MIT wrote, "It was an act of utter stupidity. To science, cyclotrons are more precious than battleships to the Navy, more difficult to procure, and of far greater value to society." *(U.S. Army Photo)*

believe you would." He turned and left, and I heard nothing more of it.

Tearing down the war machine

The problem of the demobilization and disarmament of the Japanese forces became an immediate objective as soon as the surrender ceremonies were completed. On September 2nd, the strength of these contingents totaled 6,983,000 troops, consisting of 154 army divisions, 136 brigades, and 20 important naval units. On the home islands were 2,576,000 soldiers, comprising 57 divisions, 14 brigades, and 45 regiments. The rest of Japan's armed might was scattered in a huge semicircle from Manchuria to the Solomons, and among the islands of the central and southwest Pacific.

Demobilization of the war machine was made the responsibility of the Japanese army and navy ministers in order to make full use of their technological and executive knowledge in the complex procedures of dismantling military installations and discharging personnel. General headquarters, Eighth Army, and the U.S. Navy supervised and co-ordinated this complicated and top-priority operation, but it was the Japanese themselves who performed the task.

Working with the Emperor

Shortly after my arrival in Tokyo, I was urged by members of my staff to summon the Emperor to my headquarters as a show of power. I brushed the suggestions aside. "To do so," I explained, "would be to outrage the feelings of the Japanese people and make a martyr of the Emperor in their eyes. No, I shall wait and in time the Emperor will voluntarily come to see me. In this case, the patience of the East rather than the haste of the West will best serve our purpose."

The Emperor did indeed shortly request an interview. In cutaway, striped trousers, and top hat, riding in his Daimler with the

17. Japanese war machines destroyed. There was no question as to the disposition of obvious machines of war, but sometimes rigid enforcement stood in the way of good sense. Lt. Raymond D. Mathis of Long Beach, California, told of his assignment to go into rural villages and collect all weapons; this was interpreted to include ceremonial Samurai swords. Lt. Mathis claimed that countless barrels of these prized possessions were collected and dumped at sea. Some were also repatriated by GIs and taken back to the States.

imperial grand chamberlain facing him on the jump seat, Hirohito arrived at the embassy. I had, from the start of the occupation, directed that there should be no derogation in his treatment. Every honor due a sovereign was to be his. I met him cordially, and recalled that I had at one time been received by his father at the close of the Russo-Japanese War.

He was nervous and the stress of the past months showed plainly. I dismissed everyone but his own interpreter, and we sat down before an open fire at one end of the long reception hall. I offered him an American cigarette, which he took with thanks. I noticed how his hands shook as I lighted it for him. I tried to make it as easy for him as I could, but I knew how deep and dreadful must be his agony of humiliation. I had an uneasy feeling he might plead his own cause against indictment as a war criminal. There had been considerable outcry from some of the Allies, notably the Russians and the British, to include him in this category. Indeed, the initial list of those proposed by them was headed by the Emperor's name. Realizing the tragic consequences that would follow such an unjust action, I had stoutly resisted such efforts. When Washington seemed to be veering toward the British point of view, I had advised that I would need at least one million rein-forcements should such action be taken. I believed that if the Emperor were indicted, and perhaps hanged, as a war criminal, military government would have to be instituted throughout all Japan, and guerrilla warfare would probably break out. The Emperor's name had then been stricken from the list. But of all this he knew nothing.

But my fears were groundless. What he said was this: "I come to you, General MacArthur, to offer myself to the judgment of the powers you represent as the one to bear sole responsibility for every political and military decision made and action taken by my people in the conduct of war." A tremendous impression swept me. This courageous assumption of a responsibility implicit with death, a responsibility clearly belied by facts of which I was fully

18. Gaijin Shogun and the Emperor - September 1945. This photo, taken on the occasion of the Emperor's first visit to Gen. MacArthur at the American Embassy, was widely circulated in Japan. If there were any remaining doubt as to who was in charge, the picture of the casual and relaxed General and the stiff and formal Emperor made it clear.

(Photo by Gae Faillace)

aware, moved me to the very marrow of my bones. He was an Emperor by inherent birth, but in that instant I knew I faced the First Gentleman of Japan in his own right.

The Emperor called on me often after that, our conversations ranging over most of the problems of the world. I always explained carefully the underlying reasons for occupation policy, and I found he had a more thorough grasp of the democratic concept than almost any Japanese with whom I talked. He played a major role in the spiritual regeneration of Japan, and his loyal co-operation and influence had much to do with the success of the occupation.

Reforms criticized
Russia tries for policy control

A storm of criticism in the press of our European Allies greeted my action. The leader in denunciation was Russia, which insistently demanded more participation in the occupation and control of Japan. In the United States it took the form of mild criticism of my initiating local action, instead of referring problems, even of a minor nature, for a decision from the State Department, where Far East affairs were handled by the newly appointed Under Secretary of State, Dean Acheson. The general press of the United States, however, overwhelmingly applauded and many messages from the United States were received by me in support of my actions.

But my own doubts and fears still gripped me. You do not become overnight the chief magistrate of a great state without many qualms unless your own egotistical vanity has made you a fool or a knave.

As winter approached, the Russians and the British intensified their pressure for a division of the unilateral power being exercised by the United States in the occupation. These two powers insisted

The General and Imperial Relations

Observations by Prime Minister Shigeru Yoshida on the special relationship of the General and the Emperor are significant for the reader to get a sense of the Japanese perspective.

"The Emperor first visited General MacArthur on 27 September of the year of the surrender. When I heard it was the Emperor's wish to meet the Supreme Commander for the Allied Powers, I came to the conclusion, after much thought, that such a meeting was desirable and calculated to have good results, and conveyed the wish to the General. General MacArthur answered that his position prevented him from visiting the Emperor at the Imperial Palace, but that if the Emperor would come to his residence (at the American Embassy) he would be delighted to meet His Majesty.

"At the meeting thus arranged, General MacArthur seems to have been much impressed by the Emperor and told me later that he had never met a person who behaved so nobly and naturally. This first meeting was followed by several more, and the Emperor, too, seems to have become completely at ease with the General in their conversations together. At each meeting, the tall form of the General would appear in the doorway of the American Embassy to welcome the Emperor and again to bid him farewell, towering over His Majesty.

"The General had come to have great respect for the Emperor, and even told me once that, although Japan had lost the war, the Throne was still important to the Japanese people and the reconstruction of Japan depended on the people rallying to the Imperial symbol. The fact remains that the respect and understanding shown by the General towards the Throne, and his decision to exculpate the Emperor from all and any relationship with war crimes, did more than anything else to lessen the fears of the majority of the Japanese people in regard to the Occupation and to reconcile them to it. I have no hesitation in saying that it was the attitude adopted by General MacArthur towards the Throne, more than any other single factor, that made the Occupation an historic success."[3]

---

[3] Shigeru Yoshida, The Yoshida Memoirs, Houghton Mifflin Co., Boston., 1962, pp 50-51

that Japan be divided into spheres of Allied responsibility. It was already evident that the division of Germany into separate zones of occupation had been a serious mistake. I refused to allow it. In spite of my opposition, I learned that the Allies were trying to devise some kind of a plan for a commission. I pointed out that the United States was furnishing 75 percent of the occupation force and once again voiced my most earnest objections. I also used this opportunity to underline the fact that none of these powers had been forthcoming with troops to fight the Pacific war when we needed them. We had borne the burden with Australia, and I felt strongly that we therefore should oversee the occupation and see it through a conclusion. But Secretary of State James Byrnes went to Moscow in December and met with delegates of Russia and Great Britain to discuss the matter with the two powers who were doing most of the demanding. No representative of France or China was called to this meeting.

I received no information or communication from the conference, and did not know Japan was under discussion until I saw it in the press. It was at this Moscow conference that the Far Eastern Commission was authorized. Its membership consisted of representatives of all eleven of the nations that had been at war against Japan. The United States surrendered its unilateral authority to the commission. The Far Eastern Commission itself held its meetings in Washington and transmitted its orders to an advisory group known as the Allied Council for Japan.

This consisted of four members: The United States, the British Commonwealth, China, and Soviet Russia. They met in Tokyo and were, I suppose, to oversee my supervision of the occupation.

It is difficult to reconcile this formal action taken at Moscow with President Truman's statement in his memoirs: "Anxious as we were to have Russia in the war against Japan, the experience at

Potsdam now made me determined that I would not allow the Russians any part in the control of Japan." Already the growing confusion in Washington due to a lack of co-ordination was becoming apparent.

The action at Moscow was bitterly assailed throughout the United States. The outcry became so great that, in its alarm, the Administration sought to shift the responsibility to me. On December 30, a United States State Department officer, Mr. Thomas Blake, speaking for the Far Eastern Commission, said in answer to a question: "General MacArthur saw and did not object to the new Japan control plan before it was approved at Moscow. General MacArthur was kept informed throughout the conference on matters dealing with Japan and Far Eastern affairs." This was a complete prevarication and I at once made the following announcement:

"The statement attributed to a Far Eastern Commission officer that I did not object to the new Japan control plan before it was approved at Moscow is incorrect. On October 31, before the convening of the Moscow conference, my final disagreement, to such a suggested plan, was contained in my radio to the Chief of Staff for the Secretary of State advising that the terms "in my opinion are not acceptable." Since that time my views have not been sought. Any impression which Mr. Blake's statement might imply that I was consulted during the Moscow conference is also incorrect. I have no iota of responsibility for the decisions which were made there."

The State Department thereupon acknowledged the error and confirmed the accuracy of my denial. But I realized, all too well, that the gap was growing.

The very nature of its composition and procedures eventually made the Far Eastern Commission ineffective. All four of the major powers had a veto. It took time for the commission members to convene, and it took an even longer time for them to make a decision once they had convened. As it turned out, they usually confined themselves to approving actions which the occupation had already taken on its own initiative. From the start, the Russian member tried to turn the commission into a propaganda instrument for derogatory speeches and statements designed to obstruct orderly government in Japan.

The State Department did little to counter this propaganda. The Soviet Ambassador to Washington, apparently emboldened by this silence, finally charged in an unparalleled vituperative speech, that the occupation was being mismanaged, and denounced SCAP and the Japanese government. At this period in history, Soviet rowdiness and incivility were rarely answered in kind. I knew them well and felt it a mistake not to reply in their own type of language. I therefore issued the following public reply:

> "I have noted the statement of the Soviet Ambassador before the Far Eastern Commission in derogation of American policy and action with reference to Japan. It has little validity measured either by truth or realism and can be regarded as mainly a continuation of the extraordinary irresponsibility of Soviet propaganda.

> "Its basic cause is the complete frustration of the Soviet effort to absorb Japan within the orbit of the Communistic ideology. This effort has been incessant and relentless from the inception of the occupation. It has sought by every means within its power to spread discord and dissension throughout this country reduced by the disasters of war to an economy of poverty originally

threatening the actual livelihood of the entire nation. It has hoped to so mutilate the masses that there would be imposed through the resulting despair and misery a godless concept of atheistic totalitarian enslavement. It has failed, due largely to the innate common sense and conservatism of the Japanese people, the concepts of democratic freedom implanted during the occupation and a progressive improvement in living conditions. The resulting rage and frustration have produced, as in the present instance, an unbridled vulgarity of expression which is the sure hallmark of propaganda and failure.

"For the Soviet to prate of brutality, of labor freedom and economic liberty, is enough to make Ananias blush. At least his sin was not compounded by provocative hypocrisy."

These were rough words, but words the Soviet understood. The Far Eastern Commission became little more than a debating society, and when a peace treaty was finally signed with Japan, it died a quiet death. Not one constructive idea to help with the reorientation and reconstruction of Japan ever came from the Far Eastern Commission or its satellite, the Allied Council. This latter body was, by its terms of reference, solely advisory and consultative. But it was neither the one nor the other, its sole contribution being that of nuisance and defamation.

Outline of broad reforms presented

Prince Higashi-Kuni, the Emperor's uncle and a member of the traditional ruling class, had been the prime minister of Japan from the surrender until well into October. This relationship was regarded by the Emperor as detrimental to the reforms being initiated by the occupation, and he was replaced by Baron Shidehara, one of Japan's most respected and experienced diplomats. When the newly appointed prime minister called on me I expressed to him, "I expect you to institute the following reforms in the social order of Japan as rapidly as they can be assimilated."

1. The emancipation of the women of Japan through their enfranchisement that, being members of the body politic, they may bring to Japan a new concept of government directly subservient to the well-being of the home.

2. The encouragement of the unionization of labor — that it may have an influential voice in safeguarding the working man from exploitation and abuse, and raising his living standard to a higher level.

3. The institution of such measures as may be necessary to correct the evils which exist in the child labor practices.

4. The opening of the schools to more liberal education — that the people may shape their future progress from factual knowledge and benefit from an understanding of a system under which government becomes the servant rather than the master of the people.

5. The abolition of systems which through secret inquisition and abuse have held the people in constant fear — substituting therefore a system of justice designed to afford the people protection against despotic, arbitrary and unjust methods. Freedom of thought, freedom of speech, freedom of religion must be maintained. Regimentation of the masses under the guise or claim of efficiency, under whatever name of government it may be made, must cease.

6. The democratization of Japanese economic institutions to the end that monopolistic industrial controls be revised through the development of methods which tend to insure a wide distribution of income and ownership of the means of production and

19. Japanese women emancipated. Japanese woman with child on her back changes centuries of tradition by casting a vote in the General Elections. The Meiji Constitution made no provision for rights of Japanese women; they were virtually chattel of their husbands. Gen. MacArthur gave the task of revising the constitution to a committee of the Japanese government, but after several months, it returned a revision worse than the original. In MacArthur fashion, an explicit set of objectives was presented to Baron Shidehara who replaced Prince Higashi-Kuni, the Emperor's uncle and former Prime Minister. At the top of the list was the "emancipation of women." All of the "seven freedoms" recommended by the General were adopted.

trade.

7. In the immediate administrative field take vigorous and prompt action by the government with reference to housing, feeding and clothing the population in order to prevent pestilence, disease, starvation or other major social catastrophe. The coming winter will be critical and the only way to meet its difficulties is by the full employment in useful work of everyone.

The Prime Minister was in full and enthusiastic agreement, and acted promptly and energetically. I knew better than to present this as an order from me, or to intimate that I would be disgruntled if these reforms were not made. Nothing that was good in the new Japanese government was going to be done because I imposed it, or because of fear of me and what I represented. Any change pressed home on those grounds would last only as long as I lasted. The minute I left Japan, so would the changes. These things had to come from the Japanese themselves, and they had to come because the Japanese sincerely wanted them. Some of the changes I had proposed went to the very core of the Japanese character — institutions, myths, former policy methods were in the throes of transition, and the Japanese had to understand why new institutions and new ways of doing things were desirable. I knew that the whole occupation would fail if we did not proceed from this one basic assumption — the reform had to come from the Japanese.

Our motto

During the years I was in Tokyo, I kept this concept constantly before me and before my staff.

"We must scrupulously avoid interference with Japanese acts merely in search for a degree of perfection we may not even enjoy in our own country."

Progress report

By January 1, 1946, progress of the occupation had been so favorable that I was able to issue the following statement to the people of Japan:

"A New Year has come. With it, a new day dawns for Japan. No longer is the future to be settled by a few. The shackles of militarism, of feudalism, of regimentation of body and soul, have been removed. Thought control and the abuse of education are no more. All now enjoy religious freedom and the right of speech without undue restraint. Free assembly is guaranteed. The removal of this national enslavement means freedom for the people, but at the same time it imposes upon them the individual duty to think and to act on his own initiative. The masses of Japan now have the power to govern and what is done must be done by themselves."

The General in Private

The public is in awe and wonder about the private lives of celebrities; but impressions of the public persona are so dominant, it is very difficult to imagine celebrities having a life as ordinary persons. How does a bigger-than-life person behave outside the public's gaze? Most would be surprised that the General, in private, was an unassuming person of simple tastes. He was sincerely devoted to his family and much preferred simple routines at home to pomp and ceremony.

He was a warm host when the occasion required his presence, but he did not foster 'socializing.' First, when not working, he wanted to be with his small family, and beyond that he preferred the company of a relatively small number of associates. He was most comfortable with army people, especially those with a combat background. Even low-ranking soldiers responsible for security were carefully selected combat veterans assembled into an Honor Guard Company for the General.

Former Honor Guards will attest the General was always friendly, not considering them 'fixtures.' He regularly made remarks in passing, such as, "How you doing, son,"or "Good to see you." According to military practice, a soldier wears the patch of his former outfit on his right sleeve. The General was very observant of these affiliations and would make comments about them, by unit name, to the wearer.

In his book, <u>American Caesar</u>,[4] William Manchester describes the General in the privacy of his quarters with telling words and interpretations. A portion of this is given below.

---

[4] William Manchester, <u>American Caesar</u>, Dell Publishing, N.Y., 1978, pp. 611-616

Arthur (son) was the last person MacArthur saw before retiring with Jean (his wife) and the first to greet him each morning. At 7:00 a servant would signal to four dogs sitting expectantly in a row at the foot of the hill behind the Big House (Embassy quarters).

Blackie, a cocker; Uki, a white Akita; Brownie, a Shiba terrier; and Kono, the Huffs' spaniel. Barking joyously, the four pets would race up and into the bedroom, where the Supreme Commander, his son, and the dogs would chase each other about, MacArthur shouting exultantly, Arthur shrieking, and the spaniels and terriers yelping and wagging their tails in frenzy.

Another servant would place four small dishes of egg and milk on the dining room floor, near the breakfast table. After the dogs had licked them clean they would gather around the General's table. Slipping into his old gray West Point bathrobe with the black 'A' over the heart, he would feed them scraps while he ate his most substantial meal of the day: fruit, cereal, eggs, toast, and coffee without cream but with plenty of sugar. Jean sat at the other end of the table, sipping coffee and chatting; Arthur watched his father adoringly, and the dogs patiently awaited the next part of the morning rites, MacArthur's shave. He and Arthur sang their duets while his straight razor whipped back and forth.

Then came the General's calisthenics. He never golfed, fished, hunted, cycled, jogged, or even used the embassy swimming pool, but these sitting-up exercises were vigorous workouts. The dogs knew which was the last one, and they bounded up to nuzzle him when he had finished it. Uki was Arthur's favorite — he liked to dress her up in outlandish costumes and tie hats on her head — but his father preferred Blackie. The other three pets left while he dressed, but Blackie was permitted to stay and watch. One morning Jean walked in and found him in an upholstered chair. "Oh, General," she said disapprovingly. "Look at Blackie ruining that chair. I simply will not let the dogs sit on my chairs." MacArthur replied firmly, "Jeanie, that is my chair and Blackie can get into it any time he wants to."

At eight o'clock the family gathered for prayers, the General's substitute for formal church attendance. Gibby (Mrs. Phyllis Gibbons, governess) read the service from the Anglican Book of Common Prayer, and MacArthur followed with a short passage from the Bible.

At eight-thirty Gibby rang a large brass school bell relentlessly until Arthur joined her for his first lesson of the day. Meanwhile the General had begun scanning dispatches, telling Jean which calls he wanted her to make and grumblingly placing a few himself when instant decisions were needed.

Two or three times a week he told her, before leaving for the office, to expect luncheon guests. He disliked entertaining — it usually meant he would miss his siesta — but as he told Bowers (Major Faubion, aide), "It can't be helped. Now that the war's over, every Tom, Dick and his cat's coming over. I don't want a fuss. Can't have them hoping for a visit and then leaving, saying I wouldn't see them."

The visitors would begin to arrive shortly before two o'clock. Jean, Huff, and sometimes Bowers would greet them in the huge drawing room. Often she was the only woman at the noon meal, and sometimes the only civilian; because SCAP had ruled that military officers took precedence over diplomats, many nations' representatives in

Tokyo were generals and admirals. Those expecting cocktails were disappointed. If they hinted that they were thirsty, Jean would turn to Bowers and say vaguely, "We have a little sherry, I believe, don't we, Major?" Moving quickly among them, she would deftly elicit from each why he was here and what he wanted.

After a half-hour's wait, the Cadillac would purr up the drive. "The General is coming!" she would say breathlessly, and then, as he entered the room, she would sing out, "Why, it's the General! Hi, General!" Ignoring the others he would stride quicky to her, kiss her, and then pivot toward his visitors. Having welcomed all, he would turn toward the dining room, beckon the guest of honor to his side, and rumble, "You must be hungry. I know I am."

He wasn't at all hungry. His noon and evening meals were identical and frugal: soup, salad, and coffee. But valuing his time, he wanted to get through lunch and back to his desk. He was always quietly amused at the polite jockeying for position as the visitors approached the table.

Sebald (William J. — State Department) recalls that SCAP's residence was the only establishment of the occupation which lacked protocol. 'MacArthur protocol,' as the General called it, meant that he sat at one end of the table and Jean at the other, with everyone else except the guest of honor, at his right, left to fend for themselves. Often this meant that senior officials would end up in the middle, with more vigorous juniors close to the Supreme Commander. It didn't matter; Jean would catch SCAP's eye and adroitly mention that so-and-so wanted to talk to him about such-and-such. He would break off whatever he was saying, explaining with heavy humor, "Any husband will tell you that the wife really rules the family." In this fashion everyone had a word with the host.

Over coffee he would dominate conversation in his euphonious way, analyzing the world situation and predicting what the future would bring. Then he and Jean would rise together. Often he would let her escort the guests out while he slipped away through another door. This offended some. They thought he felt himself too important for conviviality.

Few suspected that Olympian figure was painfully shy in intimate social situations, wretched in the easy give-and-take of idle conversation, jollity, and good fellowship. He vastly preferred quiet luncheons with his wife listening for the 3:00 P.M. news over a portable radio on the table, and then lying down for an hour of rest. He could hold listeners spellbound with his visions for Japan, but the kind of verbal fencing at which Franklin Roosevelt excelled — the art that all great politicians must master — was beyond MacArthur. His definition of a good meal was a quick meal. Jean had his supper on the table when he reached home, and within twenty minutes he would rise from it and enter the pantry outside the dining room, where a hole had been cut through the wall and a large motion picture screen erected. There, sitting in his red rocker, he would subject a cigar to its ritualistic circumcision, light it, and puff happily away.

During the show Jean sat on his left, Huff on his right. He would set up about fifty folding chairs, because all staff officers, servants, and even the embassy's honor guard had standing invitations to attend. Though most enlisted men continued to mock his lofty air, his stock was high with those who saw him every day. The Big House sentries (Honor Guard) had chipped in to give him an ashtray table, which stood beside the rocker, and an English tweed jacket, which on cool evenings he would slip on before the lights were dimmed for the short subjects.

MacArthur watching a newsreel, according to Norman Thompson, his projectionist of those Tokyo years, was a spectacle in itself. If an Army-Navy game was shown, he would cheer the Black Knights hoarsely, even though he had known the final score for weeks. Joseph Stalin on the screen would bring him to the edge of the rocker, tense with concentration, watching Stalin's every gesture.

Scenes of natural disasters would evoke muttered strategems for outflanking the elements, cutting off their rear, mopping them up. He liked light comedies, musicals, Westerns; any action film, particularly if Arthur was there to share it with him. On Sundays, when there were no movies, he sprawled on a divan in the Big House's small library, his smoking corncob jutting up like a listing periscope. All his life he had enjoyed reading books, particularly history, before bedtime. Now he preferred talking to Jean and listening to phonograph records. Bing Crosby was his favorite crooner. One evening she put on a new Crosby hit, "Now Is the Hour," and asked him if he could identify it. "Of course I can," he said. "It's an old Maori song." Humming, he would ascend the stairs and, like Roosevelt, fall asleep the instant his head touched the pillow. That, he told a friend, was one of the three reasons for his superb physical condition. The other two were abstemiousness — he never drank more than an occasional glass of wine during his Japanese years — and his naps.

A journalist asked Dr. Canada if the General was a good patient. "I don't know," the physician replied. "He's never sick." There was, Martin Sommers reported in the <u>Saturday</u>

<u>Evening Post</u>, "not a line on his face." George Creel of <u>Collier's</u> wrote: "I first met him in 1917 when he was a young major. He oozed energy, ability and ambition from every pore. Meeting him here in Tokyo 31 years later, it amazed me to see how few changes had been wrought by time. Still arrow-straight, and with the game flash of eye and aquilinity of features, he justified what I had been told by his personal physician. Few members of his staff, even though many years his junior, can match his physical endurance."

So remarkable was his youthful appearance that gossips claimed he wore rouge. He himself said jocularly to Sebald, "Bill, I feel like a one-horse shay. I am the only one on active service from the Military Academy prior to the class of 1909." An artist commissioned to paint his portrait confided to an acquaintance, "Of course, MacArthur has never known what to do with his hands. It is impossible to paint them because they are never still. That is why he usually stands with his hands behind his back, or otherwise contrives to hide them."

This restless energy, pent up all the more because he denied himself every pleasure outside the home, continued to fuel Japan's progress year after successful year. Still alert, still acetic, the General gradually changed from a vigorous advocate of reform to the defender of the transformations he had wrought. Like his old trench coat, which grew dirtier and dirtier as the end of the 1940s approached, and his celebrated, oil-soaked cap — which he finally, and reluctantly, allowed Huff to re-cover with part of an old uniform — the General had become a Nipponese institution.

War criminals

The Potsdam Proclamation directed specifically that, "Stern justice shall be meted out to all war criminals, including those who have visited cruelties upon our prisoners." In compliance with this directive General Yamashita was placed on trial before a military commission, found guilty and sentenced to death. He appealed to the Supreme Court of the United States, but that tribunal declined to intervene. Of the nine justices, Justices Murphy and Rutledge alone dissented. President Truman supported the action of the commission. The case came to me for review in February 1946. Here are my findings:

"It is not easy for me to pass penal judgment upon a defeated adversary in a major military campaign. I have reviewed the proceedings in vain searching for some mitigating circumstances on his behalf. I can find none. Rarely has so cruel and wanton a record been spread to public gaze. Revolting as this may be in itself, it pales before the sinister and far reaching implication thereby attached to the profession of arms. The soldier, be he friend or foe, is charged with the protection of the weak and unarmed. It is the very essence and reason for his being. When he violates this sacred trust, he not only profanes his entire cult but threatens the very fabric of international society. The traditions of fighting men are long and honorable. They are based upon the noblest of human traits — sacrifice. This officer, of proven field merit, entrusted with high command involving authority adequate to responsibility, has failed this irrevocable standard; has failed his duty to his troops, to his country, to his enemy, to mankind; has failed utterly his soldier faith. The transgressions resulting therefrom as revealed by the trial are a blot upon the military profession, a stain upon civilization and constitute a memory of shame and dishonor that can never be forgotten. Peculiarly callous and purposeless was the sack of the ancient city of Manila, with its Christian population and its countless historic

20. War criminals trials. The Potsdam Declaration was explicit about trial and punishment of those responsible for Japan's war policy and those who committed atrocities beyond the standards of wartime behavior. The most likely war criminal, other than possibly the Emperor, was Hidaki Tojo, former Premier and War Minister. He masterminded Japan's military aggression, but there was the question of the Emperor's culpability. It has been reported in Paul Manning's book, <u>Hirohito, the War Years,</u> that Tojo struck a deal whereby blame would not be directed toward the Emperor if assurances were given for the care of Tojo's family. In any case, the Emperor had Gen. MacArthur on his side. *(U.S. Army Photo)*

shrines and monuments of culture and civilization, which with campaign conditions reversed had previously been spared.

"It is appropriate here to recall that the accused was fully forewarned as to the personal consequences of such atrocities. On October 24 — four days following the landing of our forces on Leyte — it was publicly proclaimed that I would 'hold the Japanese Military authorities in the Philippines immediately liable for any harm which may result from failure to accord prisoners of war, civilian internees or civilian non-combatants the proper treatment and the protection to which they of right are entitled.'

"No new or retroactive principles of law, either national or international, are involved. The case is founded upon basic fundamentals and practices as immutable and as standardized as the most natural and irrefragable of social codes. The proceedings were guided by that primary rational of all judicial purposes — to ascertain the full truth unshackled by any artificialities of narrow method or technical arbitrariness. The results are beyond challenge.

"I approve the findings and sentence of the Commission and direct the Commanding General, Army Forces in the Western Pacific, to execute the judgment upon the defendant, stripped of uniform, decorations and other appurtenances signifying membership in the military profession."

General Homma was also brought to trial by military commission in Manila. The story of the "Death March" of Bataan, heretofore concealed from the Japanese public, had shocked Japan. The Emperor, when told of it, had stripped Homma of his commission as an officer, and of his medals and decorations. The commission found him guilty and sentenced him to death. The case came to me for final decision early in March.

Mrs. Homma asked for an opportunity to personally present her plea for clemency, and I agreed to see her. She was accompanied by one of the American officers who had defended Homma at his trial. She was a cultured woman of great personal charm. It was one of the most trying hours of my life. I told her that I had the greatest possible personal sympathy for her and understood the great sorrow of her situation. No incident, I said, could more deeply illustrate the utter evil of war and its dreadful consequences upon those like her who had little or no voice or part in it. I added that I would give the gravest consideration to what she had said. My review of the case was rendered on March 21, as follows:

"I am again confronted with the repugnant duty of passing final judgment on a former adversary in a major military campaign. The proceedings show the defendant lacked the basic firmness of character and moral fortitude essential to officers charged with the high command of military forces in the field. No nation can safely trust its martial honor to leaders who do not maintain the universal code which distinguishes between those things that are right and those things that are wrong. The testimony shows a complete failure to comply with this simple but vital standard. The savageries which resulted have shocked the world. They have become synonyms of horror and mark the lowest ebb of depravity of modern times. There are few parallels in infamy and tragedy with the brutalization of troops who in good faith had laid down their arms. It is of peculiar aversion that the victims were a garrison whose heroism and valor has never been surpassed. Of all fighting men of all time none deserved more the honors of war in their hour of final agony. The callousness of denial has never been exceeded. This violation of a fundamental code of chivalry, which has ruled all honorable military men throughout the ages in treatment of defeated opponents, will forever shame the memory of the victorious troops. I can find no circumstances of extenuation although I have searched for some instance upon which to base palliation.

"In reviewing this case I have carefully considered the minority views presented by distinguished justices of the United States Supreme Court in negation not only as to jurisdiction but as to method and merit. My action as well as the record in this case would be incomplete were I to fail the obligation as the final reviewing authority of frank expression on issues of so basic a nature. I do so from the standpoint of a member of the executive branch of the government in process of its responsibility in the administration of military justice.

"No trial could have been fairer than this one, no accused was ever given a more complete opportunity of defense, no judicial process was ever freer from prejudice. Insofar as was humanly possible the actual facts were fully presented to the commission. There were no artifices of technicality which might have precluded the introduction of full truth in favor of half truth, or caused the slanting of half truth to produce the effect of non-truth, thereby warping and confusing the tribunal into an insecure verdict. On the contrary, the trial was conducted in the unshaded light of truth, the whole truth and nothing but the truth. Those who would oppose such honest method can only be a minority who either advocate arbitrariness of process above factual realism, or who inherently shrink from the stern rigidity of capital punishment. Strange jurisprudence it would be, which for whatever reason defeated the fundamental purpose of justice — to rectify wrong, to protect right and to produce order, safety and well-being. No sophistry can confine justice to a form. It is a quality. Its purity lies in its purpose, not in its detail. The rules of war and the military law resulting as an essential corollary therefrom have always proven sufficiently flexible to accomplish justice within the strict limitations of morality.

"If this defendant does not deserve his judicial fate, none in jurisdictional history ever did. There can be no greater, more heinous or more dangerous crime than the mass destruction, under guise of military authority or military necessity, of helpless men incapable of further contribution to war effort. A failure of law process to punish such acts of criminal enormity would threaten the very fabric of world society. Human liberties, the fundamental dignities of man, the basic freedoms upon which depend the very future of civilization, all would be in peril and hazard. Soldiers of an army invariably reflect the attitude of their general. The leader is the essence. Isolated cases of rapine may well be exceptional but widespread and continuing abuse can only be a fixed responsibility of highest field authority. Resultant liability is commensurate with resultant crime. To hold otherwise would be to prevaricate the fundamental nature of the command function. This imposes no new hazard on a commander, no new limitation on his power. He has always, and properly, been subject to due process of law. Powerful as he may become in time of war, he still is not autocratic or absolute, he still remains responsible before the bar of universal justice. From time immemorial the record of high commanders, of whatever side, has been generally temperate and just. The lapses during this latest war are contrary to past trend. By universal practice such military transgressions are tried by military tribunals. No escutcheon is more unsullied of revenge and passion than that of the United States. Firmly rooted in long and noble tradition American military justice may safely be predicted to remain so.

"I approve the finding of guilt and direct the Commanding General, United States Forces in the Western Pacific, to execute the sentence."

The Potsdam Declaration also contained a purge provision requiring all Japanese who had actively engaged in militaristic and ultra-nationalistic activities prior to the war to be removed from public office and excluded from political influence. I very much doubted the wisdom of this measure, as it tended to lose the services of many able governmental individuals who would be difficult to replace in the organization of a new Japan. I put the purge into operation with as little harshness as possible, but it was the one issue in which popular support by the Japanese people was lacking. The punitive feature of such a policy always outweighs all other attributes and invariably breeds resentments which carry the germs of future discord. Many of those involved are patriots who serve their country in the light of existing conditions, and their punishment makes personal expiation for the mistakes of the nation. As soon as the peace treaty restored Japan's full sovereignty, all prohibitions against the purgees were promptly, and properly removed.

The Japanese Revolution?

If a student examined the form of the Japanese government at the beginning of the twentieth century, and rights of the people at that time, then, without knowing what took place during the interim, compared that with its status at the close of the century, what could be logically assumed?

Could it be postulated that there was a gradual evolution to democracy as the ruling class willingly gave up its power to the people? Such a proposition would not stand any test for long. Throughout the history of the world, a position of power by one group has never been freely abandoned in favor of another. One need only look at the records of the prior two centuries to find that it took a revolution, such as the American Revolution or the French Revolution, to bring about such a deep and widespread turnover of power from a ruling class to the people.

In Japan it took a monstrous and costly war to wrest the power from the ruling class only to have it fall into the hands of a former enemy. This ominous twist of fate could have been disastrous for Japan.

History has shown the most successful form of government has been democratic in principle and practice. Other forms, such as Communism, have appeal to many in principle, but in practice they inevitably become totalitarian. When there is need for sweeping change, however, the most effective form of government is a dictatorship. This cannot be disputed, but the problem for the people lies in the nature of the dictator. For the ultimate good of all the people, the dictator must be omnipotent, omniscient, and benevolent — and understand that his role is transitional. Was it by chance this fell to Gen. MacArthur, or was there a divine plan at work?

The foundation of a government is its constitution. Prior to the war Japan had a constitution, one that emerged from the Meiji Restoration, a constitution that was subverted to guarantee control by the ruling class while giving lip service to the rights of the people. Post-war this constitution was the prime target for SCAP policy changes. Since the government was largely left in place by Gen. MacArthur, to continue the administration of the country under his scrutiny, the Japanese were given the task of revising the constitution.

The General stood aside from the deliberations, allowing the political leaders and the people a full opportunity for self-determination. What he didn't know, until months later, was that "politics as usual" was controlling the process. The old power clique had managed to put its man in charge of a sham revision process. It even denigrated its purpose by selecting the name, Constitutional Problem Investigating Committee, with the implication there were some minor problems that required adjustment. Though some of the Committee members favored sweeping changes, these had been kept to a minority by the old guard.

When, after three months' work, the General viewed its recommendations, he was appalled. His plan had been scuttled by those who had no intention of giving up power and control over the people. The General did not have much to say about his state of mind over this affront when he wrote his memoirs fifteen years later, but it probably took all of that time for him to cool down, and then he wrote about the event in a statesman-like manner.

In short order, the General put to paper more explicit changes and directed his staff to "advise the Japanese" while he took up the matter with the Emperor. It was not the Emperor who was opposed; he fully supported and welcomed the proposed changes. And ironically, it was the Emperor and the

Imperial Dynasty that had the most to lose. Emperor Hirohito's intervention effectively ended the resistance of hard-liners, just as it had at the termination of the war when some insisted on carrying on the fight.

To the student, who had to postulate what might have taken place to bring about a constitutional turnabout, we can say it took a bloody, brutal lost war and the intervention of a benevolent former enemy.

Japanese constitution

Before we could really do much with the Japanese governmental system, there had to be sweeping changes in the fundamental law of the land — the constitution. The political situation in Japan was desperate. Its old Meiji constitution had been so warped in interpretation, and so deprecated in public opinion by the results of the war, that a new charter was immediately imperative if the structure of Japanese self-government was to be sustained. The choice was alien military government or autonomous civil government. The pressure for the former by many of the Allied nations was intense, accompanied by many drastic concepts designed to fracture the Japanese nation.

We could not simply encourage the growth of democracy. We had to make sure that it grew. Under the old constitution, government flowed downward from the Emperor, who held the supreme authority, through those to whom he had delegated power. It was a dictatorship to begin with, a hereditary one, and the people existed to serve it. Under these conditions, the population of Japan had no basic rights, written or unwritten. Because they had never been exposed to the idea that they might have such inherent rights, they had existed for centuries without any idea of what the possession of those rights might mean to them. The fact that they were being given something that they had never experienced promised to make the task of writing and getting acceptance for a new constitution somewhat easier than it might otherwise have been.

In my efforts for a revision of the Meiji constitution, I emphasized the point that we felt a democratic regime was essential to the new Japan, and that we could only insure such a society by having a plainly written and clearly understood statement of rights. I did not, however, try to force an American version of a Japanese constitution, and order them to adopt it. The revision had to be made by the Japanese themselves and it had to be done without coercion.

The actual task of revising the old constitution was begun in

October 1945 by a committee especially appointed by Prime Minister Shidehara. Its members were all prominent political leaders under the chairmanship of Dr. Joji Matsumoto, a member of the cabinet. The Constitutional Problem Investigating Committee, as it was called, began receiving advice almost at once from the rank and file of the Japanese people. This advice came in the form of editorials, letters, and even calls on the committee members. With no censorship in Japan any longer, the people discussed and debated the new constitution on every street corner, in every newspaper, and in every home. Even the Communist Party entered into the arguments with some zest. Everyone had his own ideas of what should go into the new document and lost no time in presenting them.

I took no part in the deliberations of the Constitutional Problem Investigating Committee, nor did any member of my staff. Because of my hands-off attitude, I was not aware of everything that went on in the committee. For three months, the work went on. It was not until the end of that period that I was informed of a split in the committee. There were two main groups: those who advocated the adoption of an extremely liberal constitution, and those who wanted as little change as possible. The committee reflected, however, the wishes of its chairman, Dr. Matsumoto, who, it developed, was an extreme reactionary and who ruled the deliberations with an iron hand. When the first draft of the new constitution was submitted in January 1946, it turned out to be nothing more than a rewording of the old Meiji constitution. The power of the Emperor was deleted not a whit. He simply became "supreme and inviolable" rather than "sacred and inviolable." And instead of incorporating a bill of rights, the new constitution took away some of the few rights that already existed. This was done by simply making them subordinate to statutory law. For example, it gave a man religious freedom, "except as otherwise provided by law." All that had to happen was for the old crowd of militarists or civil servants to get control of the Diet, and wipe out all the rights that were granted by the constitution. In other words, after three months of work, the constitution was the same as always — worse, perhaps.

I was now confronted with a time problem. Earlier, at my suggestion, the legislative body had revised the election laws, giving those who had been disenfranchised the right to vote. With this new law in effect, the government had called for a general election on April 10, 1946. I had expected that the new constitution would be finished by then and that the voting would, in fact, be a plebiscite. The way things stood after Dr. Matsumoto finished his work, the people would be voting on whether they wanted to keep the old constitution or one just like it.

Accordingly, I directed my staff to assist and advise the Japanese in the formation of an acceptable draft. The prime minister himself became active and energetic in its final preparation. The Emperor was shown the draft, and at once approved, saying that "upon these principles will truly rest the welfare of our people and the rebuilding of Japan." It was a remarkable reaction, because these principles were the very ones that were to take away the power of the imperial throne and to sign over to the state the biggest part of his personal estate and that of his family.

On March 6th, I stated to the anxious people: "It is with a sense of deep satisfaction that I am today able to announce a decision of the Emperor and the government of Japan to submit to the Japanese people a new and enlightened constitution which has my full approval."

Now began the task of seeing to it that the masses of the Japanese people had a chance to read and evaluate the new document. It was circulated throughout Japan and earnestly debated for a month. Ideas for small changes were forwarded from all sections, but by and large the people liked it and approved of it in wholehearted fashion. The only dissenters, as might have been expected, were the Communists. The government carried out a large-scale educational program in the papers and on the radio, explaining all the features and answering questions. The April election was what I had wanted — a true plebiscite. The people who had publicly committed themselves to the adoption were elected to a strong and clear majority in the new Diet.

The new constitution was not immediately adopted. In what might be called the new spirit of the times in Japan, the members of the Diet spent all summer exploring the various ramifications. When it was approved by the lower house in August, there had been a great many changes, although the basic principles were intact. The following month the House of Peers approved it. The Emperor proclaimed it the law of the land on November 3, and it went into effect in May 1947. As can be seen, more than a year and a half had gone by since work on the new document had started, and during that whole long period it had been scrutinized by the people of Japan. I know of no similar important document that ever received so much attention and open debate, including our own Constitution.

The new Japanese constitution is really an amendment to the older Meiji one. I felt that by using this particular device we could insure a continuity, and continuity is important in Japan. It is undoubtedly the most liberal constitution in history, having borrowed the best from the constitutions of many countries. From an absolute monarch, the Emperor has turned into a constitutional one, "the symbol of the state and unity of the people." The supreme power in the state is now held by the Diet. The Japanese people, for the first time in their history, enjoy the safeguards and the protection of a bill of rights. As in our own government, it provides for a separation of powers between the three branches of government. By making the courts independent of the ministry of justice, it ends one of the great evils of the former government.

There is a supreme court, and all courts are permitted to establish their own procedural rules, within the limits of the law, and they are allowed to set up their own independent budget for approval by the Diet, a fact that removes them from the influence of the legislative branch.

The form of government is a combination of the American executive system and the British parliamentary one. The prime minister serves a term of four years, but he is elected from the membership of the lower house of the legislature. If, for any reason, the prime minister is not upheld on issues that come before the Diet, he has two choices: he can resign and let the lower house elect a successor, or he can dissolve the Diet and call for new elections. This provision provides a degree of stability in the government. No group within the Diet is going to question the administration of a prime minister in an idle fashion if they are going to be forced to stand the expense of a new election campaign as a result of their capriciousness.

One of the more important amendments to the new constitution that was made as the result of the free and open debate in the Diet during the summer of 1946 was the provision for amendment by national referendum. If two-thirds of the Japanese electors decide that a change needs to be made, it goes into effect. The people themselves thus control their own constitution and are, in the final analysis, the sovereigns in their own land. One of the most interesting things about the Japanese constitution as adopted in 1946 is the fact that it has never been amended, although it has been in force for seventeen years. This speaks well for the wisdom and judiciousness that went into its final draft. Indeed, most Japanese politicians today take great pride in pointing out that they were members of the body that helped draft it or that they had worked for its adoption. It is probably the single most important accomplishment of the occupation, for it brought to the Japanese people freedoms and privileges which they had never known. And I am certain that it would never have been accomplished had the occupation been dependent on the deliberations of the Far Eastern Commission — with the Soviet power of veto!

The new Japanese constitution is not entirely free of criticism and never has been, but its critics, always extremists, do not attack the constitution on its own merits.

Peace policy

It has frequently been charged, even by those who should be better informed, that the "no war" clause was forced upon the government by my personal fiat. This is not true, as the following facts will show: Long before work was completed on the new document by Dr. Matsumoto, I had an appointment with Prime Minister Shidehara who wished to thank me for making what was then a new drug in Japan, penicillin, available in aiding in his recovery from severe illness. He arrived at my office at noon on January 24 and thanked me for the penicillin, but I noticed he then seemed somewhat embarrassed and hesitant. I asked him what was troubling him, that as prime minister he could speak with the greatest frankness, either by way of complaint or suggestion. He replied that he hesitated to do so because of my profession as a soldier. I assured him soldiers were not as unresponsive or inflexible as they are sometimes pictured — that at bottom most of them were quite human.

He then proposed that when the new constitution became final that it include the so-called no-war clause. He also wanted it to prohibit any military establishment for Japan — any military establishment whatsoever. Two things would thus be accomplished. The old military party would be deprived of any instrument through which they could someday seize power, and the rest of the world would know that Japan never intended to wage war again. He added that Japan was a poor country and could not really afford to pour money into armaments anyway. Whatever resources the nation had left should go to bolstering the economy.

I had thought that my long years of experience had rendered me practically immune to surprise or unusual excitement, but this took my breath away. I could not have agreed more. For years I have believed that war should be abolished as an outmoded means of resolving disputes between nations. Probably no living man has seen as much of war and its destruction as I had. A participant or observer in six wars, a veteran of twenty campaigns, the survivor of hundreds of battlefields, I have fought with or against the soldiers of practically every country in the world, and my abhorrence reached its height with the perfection of the atom bomb.

When I spoke in this vein, it was Shidehara's turn to be surprised. His amazement was so great that he seemed overwhelmed as he left the office. Tears ran down his face, and he turned back to me and said, "The world will laugh and mock us as impracticable visionaries, but a hundred years from now we will be called prophets."

Article 9 of Chapter 11 of the Japanese Constitution provides: "Aspiring sincerely to an international peace based on justice and order, the Japanese people forever renounce war as a sovereign right of the nation and the threat or use of force as means of settling international disputes. In order to accomplish the aim of the preceding paragraph, land, sea and air forces, as well as other war potential, will never be maintained. The right of belligerency of the State will not be recognized."

There were attacks made on this article of the constitution, especially by the cynics who said that it was against the basic nature of man. I defended it, and advocated that it be adopted. Not only was I convinced that it was the most moral of ideas, but I knew that it was exactly what the Allies wanted at that time for Japan. They had said so at Potsdam and they had said so afterwards. Indeed, my directive read, "Japan is not to have an Army, Navy, Air Force, Secret Police organization, or civil aviation." And now this had been accomplished by the Japanese themselves, not by the conquering powers.

Nothing in Article 9, however, prevents any and all necessary steps for the preservation of the safety of the nation. Japan cannot be expected to resist the overweening law of self-preservation. If attacked, she will defend herself. Article 9 was aimed entirely at eliminating Japanese aggression. I stated this at the time of the adoption of the constitution, and later recommended that in case of necessity, a defense force be established consisting of ten divisions with corresponding sea and air elements.

I stated unequivocally:

"Should the course of world events require that all mankind stand to arms in defense of human liberty and Japan comes within the orbit of immediately threatened attack, then the Japanese, too, should mount the maximum defensive power which their resources will permit. Article 9 is based upon the highest of moral ideals, but by no sophistry of reasoning can it be interpreted as complete negation of the inalienable right of self-defense against unprovoked attack. It is a ringing affirmation by a people laid prostrate by the sword, of faith in the ultimate triumph of international morality and justice without resort to the sword.

"It must be understood, however, that so long as predatory international banditry is permitted to roam the earth to crush human freedom under its avarice and violence, its high concept will be slow in finding universal acceptance. But it is axiomatic that there must be always a first in all things. The great immediate purpose Japan can serve in the confusion which overrides all of strife torn Asia is to stand out with striking and unruffled calmness and tranquility as the exemplification of peaceful progress, under conditions of unalloyed personal freedom. It can thus wield a profound moral influence upon the destiny of the Asian race.

Democracy at work

In the general election of April 10, 1946, the centuries of custom and tradition in Japan were upset by the first completely free election ever held in that country. Seventy-five percent of those eligible to vote helped to elect 466 members of the Diet. More than 13,000,000 women registered their choices for the first time, and those 13,000,000 votes changed the whole complexion of Japanese political life. Even in modern times it had been the custom of the prime minister in power to choose the majority of the Diet members who were voted on, and all of these holdovers were now voted out of office. An analysis of election returns revealed that only six of the old-line professional politicians had been sent to the legislature. Farmers, teachers, doctors, and laboring men now sat in the house once dominated by lawyers and industrialists. These were, by and large much younger people. Best of all, they included thirty-eight women.

The Japanese women were quick to take advantage of their new status under the constitution. They found jobs in professions where they had never been seen before. In the next five years, some 2000 of them even became policewomen. They took an active part in the various labor unions, a million and a half of them joining workmen's organizations. For the first time in Japanese history they fought for and secured laws giving them the same pay and same hours as men. They even asked for and received maternity leave. Until the occupation there had never been co-education in Japan except in the lower grades. This was now changed and the women received exactly the same quality of education as men. Laws concerning marriage, divorce, and adultery were revised as part of the program for equality. The old custom of contract marriages was forbidden, and concubinage was abolished. Overall the reforms accomplished by the occupation in Japan, none was more heartwarming to me than this change in the status of women.

There was much criticism of my support for the enfranchisement of women. Many Americans, as well as other so-called experts on Japan, expressed the view that Japanese women were too steeped in the tradition of subservience to their husbands to act with any degree of political independence. But I had my defenders as well. President Truman sent this message: "Tell MacArthur that I'm behind him a hundred percent, that I think he's doing an excellent job and he can be absolutely certain I'll back him to the finish." And Secretary of State Byrnes joined in: "Tell MacArthur that I think he is doing a magnificent job and that all of us back here are and will continue to support his efforts to the limit of our ability. We are all mighty proud of him."

From Herbert Hoover (former President): "I think I have a realization as perhaps no one else has of the difficulties with which you have been confronted and of the amazing service you have been to the American people." And from the eminent scholar and historian, Dr. Mary R. Beard: "There is something in General MacArthur's determination to enfranchise the women of Japan indicative of his conception of the family as the core or heart of society, and of woman as its prime guardian, which I would almost have to go back to Confucius for comparison. That he should associate the care and nutrition of the family with political democracy — and do this in his own mind, not just by pressure from another mind — gives him a standing in my mind — which is at the top of my judgment of statecraft. The whole procedure in Japan is so superior in intelligence to the occupation in Germany that General MacArthur's leadership shines with brilliant illumination."

Feeding the masses

The occupation endeavors were not confined to political reforms alone, but were far more comprehensive in scope. When the war ended in 1945, Japan was a nation completely exhausted. The cities and the factories had been gutted, the entire population of the country faced starvation. With the war, she had lost her supply of raw materials, all of which had been traditionally brought in from outside her markets, and virtually her entire merchant marine. She had no place to sell anything that she made, and no ships in which to carry her trade. Of the four home islands in the Japanese archipelago, not one was capable of feeding or supplying its population with any of the necessities of life. Only 16 percent of the land in Japan was capable of cultivation. Rice, the staple crop, was imported in large amounts, but as the war progressed the imports had ceased. Now, not even the small crops grown in Japan could be moved, as the transportation system had completely broken down. One of the first things I did was to set up our Army kitchens to help feed the people. Had this not been done, they would have died by the thousands.

I had to move fast to prevent disaster, so I immediately imported 3,500,000 tons of food from the supplies the United States Army had built up in the Pacific area. The effect upon the Japanese was electrical. The Appropriations Committee of the United States House of Representatives wanted to know how I could justify the expenditure of Army appropriations to feed our late enemy. I explained.

There is a popular misconception that the achievement of victory in modern war is solely dependent upon victory in the field. History itself clearly refutes this concept. It offers unmistakable proof that the human impulses which generated the will to war, no less than the material sinews of war, must be destroyed. Nor is it sufficient that such human impulses merely yield to the temporary shock of military defeat. There must be a complete spiritual reformation such as will not only control the defeated generation, but will exert a dominant influence upon the generation to follow as well. Unless this is done, victory is but partially complete and offers hope for little more than an armistice between one campaign and the next. The great lesson and warning of experience is that victorious leaders of the past have too often contented themselves with the infliction of military defeat upon the enemy power without extending that victory by dealing with the root causes which led to war as an inevitable consequence.

Under the responsibilities of victory the Japanese people are now our prisoners, no less than did the starving men on Bataan become their prisoners when the peninsula fell. As a consequence of the ill treatment, including starvation of Allied prisoners in Japanese hands, we have tried and executed the Japanese officers upon proof of responsibility. Can we justify such punitive action if we ourselves, in reversed circumstances but with hostilities at an end, fail to provide the food to sustain life among the Japanese people over whom we now stand guard within the narrow confines of their home islands? To cut off Japan's relief supplies in this situation would cause starvation to countless Japanese — and starvation breeds mass unrest, disorder and violence. Give me bread or give me bullets.

I got bread.

Fiscal responsibility

We fed the Japanese, but we didn't intend to feed them forever. I directed my staff to work out the plans we needed to make Japan self-sufficient as soon as it was humanly possible. We had to rebuild the factories that had been bombed. We had to put the machinery in working order. We had to get the trains running, and float some kind of merchant marine. We had to get the telegraph and radio and newspapers in operation. And last of all, we had to get the overses trade revived. One of the biggest tasks was to give Japan a balanced budget.

I've never seen a more tangled financial mess than that into which the Japanese government had fallen by the end of the war. Most of the money had gone to support the war effort. No one really knew how much. The taxes were incredibly heavy, and for some of the poor people amounted to confiscation of everything they had. There had been a tax rebellion in the later stages of the war. Some tax collectors were too frightened to even try to collect any longer. We decided to start over, and to that end we brought in tax experts from the United States government to completely revise the tax laws and methods of collection. When this revision was finally passed, it worked well. And I required the Japanese government to live within its income. The Japanese leaders and people responded splendidly to these budgetary provisions, and for my entire administration the fiscal policies of the country were an admirable model for the rest of the world to follow. The public debt of Japan was less than $2 billion at the time I left the country.

21. East meets West. Not far from GHQ, an army master sergeant engages a pretty Japanese girl in conversation. The shy Japanese were overwhelmed by the friendly "round eyes," and many soon welcomed their attention. Gen. MacArthur was open-minded about fraternization, recognizing that the inevitable was not a bad thing.

Fraternization

When it came to the basics, involving attitudes and interests of the common soldier, Gen. MacArthur was always correct in his assessments, and what could be more basic to the soldier than sex, especially after living in a deprived state? On many occasions his staff of advisors were not in his camp, but the General had no reservations about turning a deaf ear to others when his instincts guided him.

About fraternization he said, "Sometimes my whole staff was lined up against me, but I knew what I was doing. After all, I had more experience. And most of the time I was right."[5] His brief tour in occupied Germany after WWI had convinced him that banning social contacts with the defeated population was poor policy. "Soldiers will be soldiers," he said. He thought GIs were more interested in companionship than sex, anyhow, though he wasn't against that either. During one of his drives through the capital he saw an American soldier embracing a Japanese girl in a doorway, fondling her breasts as she reached between his thighs. "Look at that," the General said to Major Faubion Bowers. "They keep trying to get me to stop all of this Madam Butterflying around. I won't do it. My father told me never to give an order unless I was certain it would be carried out. I wouldn't issue a non-fraternization order for all the tea in China."

And fraternize they did. Certainly there were a many GIs devoted to wives or sweethearts at home, but the majority of the unattached young men had sex on their mind and made the most of it. Much has been said about the sexual revolution of the 1960s; it wasn't entirely original. However, a significant differ-

---

[5] William Manchester, <u>American Caesar</u>, Dell Publishing, New York, 1978, p. 548

ence between the sixties phenomenon and the behavior of GIs in Japan was the generally monogamous nature of the later. The impetus for this came mostly from the Japanese girls them-selves, they were very critical of 'cho-cho' boys, referring to the butterfly that flits from flower to flower. Of course, prostitution was also widespread, but these girls specialized in the 'quick-ee,'and generally did not form lasting relationships. The General said that GIs were more interested in companionship than sex; while this may have been overstated, it was true.

After GIs experimented a bit with prostitutes, they often decided that sex alone was not all that satisfying, and they sought companionship. With patience and diligent application of mating skills, they could find Japanese girls who were interest-ed in a relationship. They could be found in public places or where they worked in support of Occupation operations, PXs, clubs, dance halls, restaurants, and shops. Usually, families of these girls depended on them for financial assistance, not only from their day jobs, but also if they elected to co-habit, or 'shack-up,' a word that was popularized with the Occupation, a portion of the money or goods the girls received from their boyfriends went to the family.

GIs by the thousands fell in love with the comely, sensitive, and satisfying Japanese girls. For many it was the first time they experienced a sexual relationship at all, or one of any duration. Folks at home may have had difficulty understanding how this was possible with people of another race, for the GI was not dri-ven by lust alone, he saw the musime (moos-a-may; translated girl; colloquialized unflatteringly as 'moose' by GIs) as a wor-thy object of his affection and more.

Over 25,000 GIs married Japanese during the Occupation, but unfortunately, like marriages of other young people, many were not to last. Ill-conceived marriages fell apart shortly after the servicemen returned to the States with their 'war-brides.' Many difficulties were encountered as the couples tried to assimilate in American society. Divorce seemed an easy answer. Some of the rejected Japanese girls returned to their homeland. Some found others of similar plight and, with mutual support, they made a home for themselves in America. There are thousands of happy stories also, of couples who experienced the hardships of a mixed race marriage in a less tolerant society — along with the usual challenges of marriage, but their love was true and strong, carrying them through the adversities. The author is proud to note that there are many such success stories among his fellow Honor Guard members.

Here's one GI's story, we'll call him Bud, and his trial of a youthful romance. He was smitten by Masako, a beautiful girl with intelligence, poise and charm. She modeled for a department store and worked at a taxi dance hall. Bud was tipped off about her by a relative, a Japanese houseboy who worked at Bud's billet in the Finance Building. He told Bud that her boyfriend was suddenly shipped back to the States and that she might be interested in another. With nothing better to do, he decided to look for her at the Club Oasis Dance Hall. This club was in a basement on the Ginza, approximately in the location of the present Matsuzakaya department store.

The club was quite large, with a low ceiling which later in the evening would capture a cloud of blue tobacco smoke that would have downed the less hearty. To the left, by the entry, was a cashier's booth where dance tickets were purchased. Dance tickets were about ten cents each, but it took ten for a dance, and if the patron wasn't alert his dance partner might cop a few extra from his string. A large bottle of beer was 100 yen, or about thirty-five cents at the time. Much after payday, on a limited budget, beer was more affordable than the dancing, so one had

22. Masako X. This 21-year-old girl, like countless others, did what she could to earn her living and help support her family during the Occupation. Masako modeled, designed clothes, worked in a dance hall, helped her mother at a small sake bar, and had a G.I. boyfriend.

ample opportunity to inspect the 'hostesses.' They stood along the left wall, not all great lookers, but someone for everyone. To the discerning eye it didn't take long to pick out the more exceptional girls; they didn't have to wait long for a partner.

To write about a dance hall, the author must say something about the music. The musicians were all relatively young Japanese with just enough skill to read music or follow a popular tune with something recognizable, but usually not very well. What was more akimbo was the singing accompaniment, as few Japanese had the skill to pronounce the words they uttered. There may have been singers with good voices, but if so, they were lost in the mangling of the language. As bad as it might have been however, it was great nonetheless to hear popular American music and have the opportunity to dance with pretty girls.

As for Masako, the unknown face Bud associated with one of the popular beauties, he started his search by dancing with an ordinary-looking hostess, asking her to point out the girl whose full name he provided. The first evening was wasted as she was not working. When he returned another night, he was not optimistic and contemplated finding another prospect. But when Masako was pointed out to Bud, he felt that kah-thump in the chest and, as they now say, 'he was history.'

She didn't go for him right away; in fact, after depleting most of his funds on dance tickets, Bud had the impression she didn't think much of him at all. Meanwhile, his buddy Rod, also from the Honor Guard, was making headway with another girl who was a close friend of Masako's. With Rod's help they arranged a daytime date for the foursome, during which Masako agreed to see Bud again, alone. He was soaring with excitement, oh, young love, oh, those carnal thoughts. They met an afternoon on the Ginza and walked from one end to the other, window shopping and stopping along the way for refreshments. She looked beautiful and was very stylishly dressed, uncommonly so for a Japanese girl at that time. He learned later that she modeled and designed her own clothes from American magazines. Her English was fair and she helped him with Japanese. It was a great time, during which, in the back of Bud's mind, he was mentally struggling with how he was going to get her to the futon. He finally mustered the nerve to say, "I know a nice hotel near here." (They were all over the place.) She laughed and said, "Is that all you want?" To salvage his ego, he laughed with her and didn't press the matter.

On subsequent dates, during which Bud was experiencing ever intensifying hormonal attacks, Masako took him to her family's residence outside Tokyo, in Denenchofu, where he met her sister and father. He later met her mother, a very friendly warm-hearted mama-san, who operated a small sake bar in Oimachi. All this time Bud was romancing to his utmost with no success. Masako then told him she wouldn't go to a hotel, only to a place of their own. This was scary concept to a twenty-year old who had no thoughts of a committed relationship, but his intense affection and rising level of hormones convinced him. Simply put, they agreed to 'shack-up.'

This arrangement meant leasing a room and buying furnishings. It was big dough on a corporal's pay, but he had a little money in the States from savings while in Korea. His story to his parents was, he was going in halves on buying a car with his buddy, Rod, a complete fabrication, but Rod did have a motorcycle which gave Bud the idea. They found a place in Oimachi, a room in a small Japanese home, with access to a kitchen and toilet. For bathing there was a public bath about two blocks away.

Across from the alleyway leading to their place, a high ranking officer, Admiral Joy, SCAP Chief of Staff, lived in a large residence. On occasion Bud had to wait for the Admiral's car to pass, where he was in full view and quite noticeable — an American dressed in kimono and clogs holding a bathing bowl and towel, among a group of Japanese. On other days the Admiral would see Bud in full Honor Guard regalia outside his office at the Dai Ichi Building. On one occasion he looked at Bud with a curious stare, was about to say something, then just smiled and shook his head.

For about a year it was a grand romance as Bud spent most of his free time with Masako when she was not working. The futon was well used. Occasionally, he would sit at the sake bar while Masako helped her mother; the patrons seemed to accept the company of the odd American. They went to Japanese movies he didn't understand, occasionally to American movies at the Ernie Pyle Theater, across the side street from the Imperial Hotel, to the beach at Atami, and a mad time at a hot springs hotel there, shopping excursions for Masako to find fabric or trimmings for her dresses, and more.

It was great, but it went sour mostly due to Bud's juvenile jealousy. Masako continued to work at the Club Oasis, where he frequently looked on as she plied her trade. Bud thought she got too friendly with her customers. She told him that if he gave her enough money, she would quit her job, but that wasn't possible on his pay and didn't agree with him. Although it was a practical matter for her, he believed she was only interested in his money. They began fighting, especially when he had overdrunk the beer, and within a month before Bud's leaving for the States, they parted less than friendly.

After a four-year courtship with a local hometown girl, while completing college on the GI Bill, Bud married. He shared some of the stories and pictures from Japan, including his Japanese girlfriend Masako, with his wife and she took it with good grace, not concerned about an old affair. But there is a sequel to the story, albeit mysterious.

In the late 80s, Bud and his wife were living in Tokyo where he established an operation for a Canadian company. Frequently on weekends they would take the train into shopping areas of central Tokyo, for shopping and sightseeing. On one Sunday afternoon they were returning to their stop at Shinagawa Station, when Bud noticed an attractive Japanese woman who was standing across from where they were seated. She looked directly at him, which is very unusual in Japan. There was a resemblance he couldn't quite place, but then it occurred to him. He said to his wife, "Look casually at the woman by the door, she looks like my old girlfriend might look today." As they traveled Bud noticed she glanced at him a couple of times and his curiosity began to rise. Since Oimachi was only a couple stops further on the same line, Bud suggested that they go there to check out the local department store. His wife gave him a reproving smile and agreed.

They got off when the train stopped at Oimachi, and so did the mystery woman! As she turned away, she looked at Bud again over her shoulder. By this time, the coincidence upon coincidence was beginning to raise his hackles. They lost her in the crowd as they proceeded to the department store for some 'window shopping.' Later as they walked back to the station, Bud took a route that would bring them past the former location of Masako's mother's sake shop. As they turned the corner, she was there, standing about where the shop had been. Bud literally went into shock, he exchanged glances with the Japanese woman and walked by, hardly breathing. He said to his wife, "That must be her." He wife asked him to go back to talk to her, but he couldn't ... he's still not sure why.

23. Black market. Another inevitable result of a disrupted economy, where many goods were scarce yet somehow available, is a black market. Some major problems did arise that were subject to military justice, but the average GI's involvement was relatively innocent. Goods purchased in a PX could readily be sold to a back street merchant for twice or more their cost. Strictly speaking, this was illegal, but such minor transactions were not worth policing. For example, a carton of cigarettes could be bought for one dollar in the PX and sold on the street for about 2000 yen, which was more than enough for a night on the town. Military scrip, as shown, was used for legitimate transactions.

Free enterprise

I experienced some trouble in establishing a free enterprise system. For many decades a monopolistic control of the means of production and distribution had been exercised by the so-called Zaibatsu — about ten Japanese families who practiced a kind of private socialism. They controlled 90 percent of all Japanese industry. These great trusts were partially dissolved and a truly competitive free enterprise system inaugurated. We did not expropriate the stock in these industries without compensation. The stockholders, practically all belonging to the big families, were paid off. The main thing was that their influence was broken.

The labor movement is tested

Japanese labor had never had the right of collective bargaining until the occupation gave it to them. It was one of the first reforms I made. Laboring men throughout the empire were quick to take advantage of this new right. By 1947 there were approximately 25,000 unions in Japan and over 5,000,000 workingmen belonged to them. The labor front soon became divided into a rightist and a leftist group. Manifestations of labor unrest promptly took forms that were peculiar to Japan. A chorus line went on half-strike by only kicking half as high as usual. One railroad union protested by blowing the whistles on all the trains in Japan for one minute at the same time. I tried to encourage a labor leadership that would have the common sense to understand that labor's conflicts were never confined to the interests of workers and management alone, but that the interest of the general public was equally great. But due to trouble with the Communists, I was only partially successful.

We had trouble with the Communists in the labor movement. They obtained control of some unions and eventually called a general strike. It was a difficult situation for me. I did not want to stand in the way of newly organized laborers attempting to assert their rights, but I was not going to let a few Communist leaders use the strike as a political weapon and in so doing wreck the whole econ-

24. Private enterprise. A Japanese couple is seen working industriously in their home, assembling toys. GIs had a saying, "If you throw a beer can away, you can find it made into a toy on the Ginza by the next day." This was literally true as many Japanese scavenged whatever they could find to create something valuable for sale. Some businesses that started in home quarters have grown into mega-businesses of today, i.e., Sony.

omy. It became necessary to use the powers of my office for the general good. I therefore issued the following edict:

"Under the authority vested in me as Supreme Commander for the Allied Powers, I have informed the labor leaders whose unions have federated for the purpose of conducting a general strike that I will not permit the use of so deadly a social weapon in the present impoverished and emaciated condition of Japan, and have accordingly directed them to desist from the furtherance of such action. I have done so only to forestall the fatal impact of such extreme measures upon an already gravely threatened public welfare. Japanese society today operates under the limitations of war, defeat and Allied occupation. Its cities were laid waste, its industries are almost at a standstill, and the great masses of its people are on little more than a starvation diet.

"A general strike, crippling transportation and communications, would prevent the movement of food to feed the people and of coal to sustain the essential utilities, and would stop such industry as is still functioning. The paralysis which would inevitably result might reduce large masses of the Japanese people to the point of actual starvation, and would produce dreadful consequences upon every Japanese home, regardless of social strata, or direct interest in the basic issue. Even now, to prevent actual starvation in Japan, the people of the United States are releasing to them large quantities of their own food resources. The persons involved in the threatened general strike are but a small minority of the Japanese people. Yet this minority might well plunge the great masses into a disaster not unlike that produced in the immediate past by the minority which led Japan into the destruction of war."

As I expected, the Japanese people, including the rank and file of labor, understood what I was talking about. There was no general strike.

The Communists did not give up, however. They infiltrated

the key transportation unions, which were primarily operating in government owned and operated industries. I looked upon this as a threat to the whole government, and I advised the leaders of the government to bring all workers into the civil service. A law was passed to this effect. Immediately, people in other countries condemned the action and described me as an enemy of labor. Even people in the United States government criticized the legislation. I asked the United States Civil Service Commission to review the act, and they wrote me that it was "decidedly more liberal than the statutes pertaining to the United States Civil Service System." That ended the Communists as a factor in Japanese labor.

Economic realities

I stated Japan's economic situation at that time as follows: "The Japanese are a proud, sensitive, and industrious race. They ask no alms from anyone and expect none. They seek only the inalienable right to live. The alternatives are as simple as they are few. Either Japan must have access to the raw materials needed to sustain its industrial plant and to markets in which to dispose of its manufactured products, or it must have provisions for voluntary migration of large masses of its population to less populated areas of the world. Either solution rests upon the good will and statesmanship of others. Lacking such good will and if statesmanship fails, Japan would be forced to desperation or to death. Men will fight before they starve."

Spiritual renewal

Japan underwent a spiritual recovery along with its economic and political changes. For centuries the Japanese people, unlike their neighbors in the Pacific basin — the Chinese, the Malayans, the Indians, and others, have been students and idolaters of the art of war and the warrior caste. They were the natural warriors of the Pacific. Unbroken victory for Japanese arms convinced them of their invincibility, and the keystone to the entire arch of their civilization became an almost mythological belief in the strength and wisdom of the warrior caste. It permeated and controlled not only all the branches of the government, but all branches of life — physical, mental, and spiritual. It was interwoven not only into all government process, but into all phases of daily routine. It was not only the essence, but the warp and woof of Japanese existence.

Control was exercised by a feudalistic overlordship of a mere fraction of the population, while the remaining millions, with a few enlightened exceptions, were abject slaves to tradition, legend, mythology, and regimentation. During the progress of the war, these millions heard of nothing but Japanese victories. Then they suddenly felt the concentrated shock of total defeat; their whole world crumbled. It was not merely the overthrow of their military might — it was the collapse of a faith, it was the disintegration of everything they had believed in and lived by and fought for. It left a complete vacuum, morally, mentally, and physically. And into this vacuum flowed the democratic way of life. The falseness of their former teachings, the failure of their former leadership, the tragedy of their past faith were infallibly demonstrated in actuality and realism.

A spiritual revolution ensued which almost overnight tore asunder a theory and practice of life built upon 2000 years of history and tradition and legend. Idolatry for their feudalistic masters and the warrior class was transformed into hatred and contempt, and the hatred and contempt for their foe gave way to honor and respect. This revolution of the spirit among the Japanese people represents no thin veneer designed to serve the purpose of the present. It represents an unparalleled convulsion in the social history of the world.

Freedom of religion

Christianity, of course, is not the oldest of man's faiths. Although I was brought up as a Christian and adhere entirely to its teachings, I have always had a sincere admiration for many of the basic prin-

111

ciples underlying the Oriental faiths. Christianity does not differ from them as much as one would think. There is little conflict between the two, and each might well be strengthened by a better understanding of the other. I asked for missionaries, and more missionaries.

From the beginning I guaranteed that every Japanese could worship as he wished. I knew however that true religious freedom could never be achieved in Japan until drastic revision was made in the ancient, backward, state-controlled subsidized faith known as Shintoism. The Emperor, himself, was the High Priest of Shinto and, by the precepts of a mythological hold over from primitive times, derived his spiritual power from his imperial ancestors who had become gods. The Japanese people were told that the Emperor was divine himself and that the highest purpose of every subject's life was death in his service. The militarists who had led Japan into war had used this religion to further their efforts, and the state still subsidized it.

In November 1945, while making no theological attack, I ordered state subsidization to cease. On New Year's Day, 1946, the Emperor, without any suggestion or discussion with me, issued a rescript in which he publicly renounced his own divinity. The Emperor's statement read:

"We stand by the people and we wish always to share with them in their moments of joys and sorrows. The ties between us and our people have always stood upon mutual trust and affection. They do not depend upon mere legends and myths. They are not predicated on the false conception that the Emperor is divine and that the Japanese people are superior to other races and fated to rule the world."

I publicly commented at once:

"The Emperor's New Year's message pleases me very much. By it he undertakes a leading part in the democratization of his people. He squarely takes his stand for the future along liberal lines. His action reflects the irresistible influence of a sound idea. A sound idea cannot be stopped."

After this, Shinto priests were permitted to continue their teachings so long as church and state were separated.

Whenever possible, I told visiting Christian ministers of the need for their work in Japan. "The more missionaries we can bring out here, and the more occupation troops we can send home, the better." The Pocket Testament League, at my request, distributed 10 million Bibles translated into Japanese. Gradually, a spiritual regeneration in Japan began to grow.

Educational reform

The educational system when I arrived in Japan gave me deep concern. The Japanese practiced central control over the schools. There was no such thing as a local school board or superintendent. A ministry of education in Tokyo bought standard textbooks in everything, and distributed them throughout the country. These textbooks were filled with militaristic and anti-American items, and all were under the control of Tokyo. As a matter of fact, up until the time of the occupation, the schools, newspapers, theater, radio, and motion pictures were all part of an official propaganda machine, and can be said to have existed for the purpose of "thought control" rather than for their own intrinsic purpose.

A free people can exist only without regimentation and the publication of textbooks was promptly taken out of the control of the Ministry of Education. I put the Japanese publishing industry on a competitive basis for the first time in the preparation and printing of school textbooks. No texts were forced upon them, but the books had to show that the previous militaristic, ultra-nationalistic propaganda was absent. In the first year of the occupation, the schoolchildren of Japan, for the first time in several generations, studied from textbooks that were primarily educational. I believe the number of such new textbooks distributed in that time was something over 250,000,000.

Uncensored textbooks are of little value without uncensored teachers. I wanted the teachers to have complete academic freedom, and I moved to insure this with my directive to the Ministry of Education. "Teachers and educational officials who have been dismissed, suspended or forced to resign for liberal or anti-militaristic opinions or activities," I said, "will be declared immediately eligible for reappointment. Discrimination against any student, teacher or educational official on grounds of race, nationality, creed, political opinion or social position, will be prohibited. Students, teachers and educational officials will be encouraged in unrestricted discussion of issues involving political, civil and religious liberties."

After the new system had been in effect for some time, we tested our efforts, and the results were extremely gratifying. There was a complete reorientation in the outlook of Japanese children. In a society that had been almost completely militaristic in outlook only a few years before, it was found that most children were now most interested in the professions and the workaday world. As a matter of fact, among hundreds, there was only one child who expressed an interest in an army or navy career. He wanted to be General MacArthur! So I knew I had at least one faithful follower.

Health of the nation in peril

Health was another pressing problem. It had always been a popular conception in the United States that the Japanese were far advanced in the field of medicine and hygiene. This was not at all the case. Diseases such as smallpox, diphtheria, and typhoid cases which had all but disappeared in the United States by 1920 were still epidemic in Japan in 1945. Tuberculosis was almost a national scourge. In investigating these amazing statistics, it was not hard to find the reasons. At the close of the war, in all of Japan there were only two sanitary engineers. And the lack of personnel to

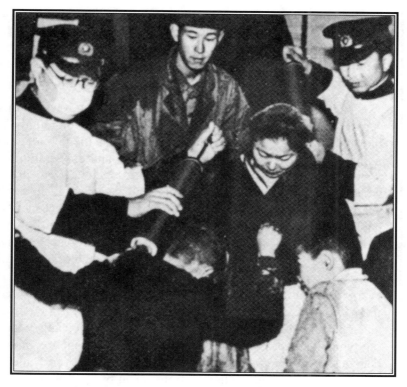

25. Public health problems. This picture shows public health officials dusting Japanese civilians with DDT powder, an excellent remedy for lice, fleas, and other bodily infestations. Gen. MacArthur was surprised to find that diseases that had been under control in the U.S. for decades — smallpox, diptheria, typhoid, cholera, and tuberculosis, were still running rampant in Japan. The General advised the prime minister to set up some kind of government health department in the cabinet, which led to the formation of the Ministry of Health and Welfare. With the help of American medical authorities, over one hundred million inoculations were made, which was estimated to save over two million lives in the first two years of the Occupation.

handle the country's hygienic problems made the situation in a bombed-out country almost chaotic. I sought immediately to improve this situation. I suggested to the prime minister that he set up some kind of a health department in the cabinet, something that Japan had never had.

The Ministry of Health and Welfare was the outgrowth of this suggestion, and today its activities are felt in every community in the land. I also suggested that all schools educate their children in public health. This was done. With the help and cooperation of American medical authorities, the Japanese people were given what amounted to a mass inoculation and vaccination. In three years, we vaccinated 70,000,000 for smallpox and succeeded in curbing the disease which had been rampant. We tested the population for tuberculosis, and administered 23,000,000 vaccinations for that disease. Seventy-nine percent of the tuberculosis cases in Japan disappeared. By systematically inoculating residents of every hamlet and city in the nation against diphtheria, we reduced the number of cases by 86 percent in three years. By a co-ordinated program of inoculation and education, we practically wiped out typhoid and paratyphoid. Through education alone we almost conquered dysentery. Our greatest triumph was over cholera, which we completely eradicated from Japan by the beginning of 1947. It was the estimate of my medical officers that we had saved 2,000,000 lives with these health measures in the first two years of the occupation. With the dreadful loss of lives in the war fresh in my mind, these statistics brought much comfort to my soul.

Land reform

One of the most far-reaching accomplishments of the occupation was the program of land reform. Japan's feudalistic regime was most evident in the matter of landholding. As late as the end of the war, a system of virtual slavery that went back to ancient times was still in existence. Most farmers in Japan were either out-and-out serfs, or they worked under an arrangement through which the landowners extracted a high percentage of each year's crops. The

26. Peasant farmers become landowners. This photo shows rural farmers, in simple cartoons, how they can acquire the land they work. Gen. MacArthur believed that the men and women who worked the land should have the opportunity to own it and took steps to have legislation passed which could make this possible. Under the new program, the government bought large farmlands, at then fair market prices, and sold small parcels to resident farmers under favorable conditions. This freed hundreds of thousand of farmers from feudal serfdom, providing economic security and the dignity of self-determination.

occupation was only a few months old when I attacked this problem. I felt that any man who farmed the land should, by law, be entitled to his crops, that there should be an end to sharecropping, and that even more fundamental, perhaps, was the need to make land itself available to the people. Under the system then in use it was practically impossible for a farmer to buy his own land.

I set up a natural resources section in the headquarters, and this group advised the Japanese government. Over the next few years, a series of laws was passed under which the government bought up land at fair prices from the big absentee landlords, and made it available to the tenants on long-term installment purchasing plans. By 1950, more than 5,000,000 acres had been redistributed. In this period, Japan was transferred from a feudal economy of impoverished serfs and tenant farmers into a nation of free landholders. More than 89 percent of all arable land in Japan was controlled by the people who lived on it. The redistribution formed a strong barrier against any introductions of Communism in rural Japan. Every farmer in the country was now a capitalist in his own right.

End of the abusive police state

The police problem in Japan was an extraordinarily difficult one to solve. One school of thought was that Japan lent itself to the maintenance of public order by a centralized police system; this was contrasted with the view that local responsibility for exercise of the police power was inherently an aspect of local autonomy, provided for by the new constitution, without which local government could not become dynamic and grow. I told the prime minister:

"It has been a dominant characteristic of modern totalitarian dictatorships, as it was in Japan's feudalistic past, to establish and maintain a strongly centralized police bureaucracy headed by a chief executive officer beyond the reach of popular control. Indeed, the strongest weapon of the military clique in Japan in the

27. Gen. MacArthur off to lunch — May 10, 1947. The general is shown following his daily ritual, leaving the GHQ operations headquarters at the Dai Ichi Building. He is accompanied by Col. Wheeler (on right). Honor Guards present in the picture are Lt. David E. Lindeneau (facing), who later died in the Korean War, Sgt. Weiner and Pfc. Vito Mitkus. The Dai Ichi Seimei Life Insurance Company, owner and occupant of the building, maintains Gen. MacArthur's office in its original state as an Historical Exhibition Room. The building is in the Marunouchi section of downtown Tokyo, across the street from the Imperial Palace grounds. Parked at the curb is the General's "big car," a postwar Cadillac which replaced the prewar model he brought from the Philippines in 1945. *(Photo courtesy of Ken Eddy)*

decade prior to the war was the absolute authority exercised by the national government over the 'thought police' and the Kempei-Tai extending down to prefectural levels of government. These media enabled the military to spread a network of political espionage, and suppress freedom of speech, of thought."

It should be borne in mind that in the final analysis police power in the preservation of law and order in a democratic society does not attain its maximum strength through oppressive controls imposed upon the people from above, but rather does it find the infinitely greater strength in the relationship of a servant of, and answerable directly to, the people. Thereby and thereby alone may it encourage respect for the people's laws through confidence and paternalistic pride in the police as the law enforcement agency of the people themselves.

The Diet, after a long debate, passed a law providing that "local public entities shall have the right to manage their property affairs and administration and to enact their own regulations within the law." It was a knotty problem then and is still a matter of argument in Japan.

I will always take the utmost satisfaction in having introduced the writ of habeas corpus into Japan. It was one of the laws which were passed to bolster the bill of rights in the new constitution. This same basic right had been brought to the Philippines by my father in 1901. It is a unique provision in Anglo-Saxon jurisprudence that a great many peoples of the world still do not possess. It moves me deeply that my family helped to bring this guarantee against arbitrary arrest to the Far East as a safeguard for Asian peoples.

The superlative staff that made it work

In these various reforms, numerous officials of the occupation distinguished themselves: Whitney, Marquat, Willoughby, Sams, Dodge, Moss, Schenk, Shoup, Kades, and many others.[6] Without their special talents and skills, little could have been accomplished. And the Japanese themselves truly earned the respect and faith of men of good will everywhere. Under their able Prime Minister Yoshida, they rose, in their own merit, from the ashes of destruction to a vibrant nation firmly rooted in immutable concepts of political morality, economic freedom, and social privilege evolved from a blend of ideas and ideals of the West and their own hallowed traditions and time-honored cultures.

For example, an editorial in The New York Times said: "Japan is the one bright spot in Allied military government. General MacArthur's administration is a model of government and a boon to peace in the Far Fast. He has swept away an autocratic regime by a warrior god and installed in its place a democratic government presided over by a very human emperor and based on the will of the people as expressed in free elections." It noted that the Russian delegate to the Allied Council for Japan did not share this view. The Soviet viewpoint was termed "a definite policy, the purpose of which is an attempt at Communist propaganda inspired from outside Japan and in violation of Potsdam terms. The odd feature in this picture is the more or less open support of these tactics by the Chinese and British delegates. It may be they hope to back up demands of their governments for stripping Japan economically in the same way that Russia stripped Korea."

---

[6] Notably absent from this list is the name of William J. Sebald, a man of incredible talent who was fluent in the Japanese language and experienced from pre-war days in Japanese law. However, Sebald was at GHQ as a member of the State Department, which was often at odds with the General. Sebald's contribution to the Occupation effort should not be minimized. For more information see his book, With MacArthur in Japan, W.W. Norton & Co., New York, 1965.

Restoring national pride

In the spring of 1947, I authorized the display of the national flag of Japan. There was a great resurgence throughout the nation of self-respect and self-confidence. Kozaemon Kimura, minister of agriculture and forestry, following a conference with the Emperor, commented as follows: "With tears in his eyes, the Emperor expressed his appreciation of General MacArthur's attitude and interest in the reconstruction of Japan. He said the Japanese people think of him as Kamikaze (divine influence). Admiral Perry opened the door of Japan to America. General MacArthur has opened the heart of America to Japan."

Power to the people

Sometime after the adoption of the constitution, the public prosecutor of the city of Tokyo dismissed charges against five individuals who had publicly criticized the Emperor. This was a unique experience for the Japanese people, and I took the opportunity to point out that neither the President of the United States nor the King of England is protected by any special laws. If the President of the United States is assassinated, his murderer is treated exactly as though he had slain a private citizen.

The decision (I said) is a noteworthy application of the fundamental concept that all men are equal before the law, that no individual in Japan, not even the Emperor, shall be clothed in legal protection denied the common man. It marks a true understanding of the lofty spirit of the new National Charter which secures to all the right to freely discuss all issues, political, social and economic of concern to the people. For the free interchange of ideas, the free expression of opinion, the free criticism of officials and institutions is essential to the life and growth of popular government. Democracy is vital and dynamic, but cannot survive unless all citizens are free to speak their minds. The legal protection accorded an

28. Restoring national pride. At the commencement of the Occupation, all symbols of the national government were removed from public display, as they were considered to be emblematic of the defeated enemy. In the Spring of 1947, Gen. MacArthur, sympathetic to the yearnings of the populace, authorized the display of the national flag. A cabinet minister reported, "With tears in his eyes the Emperor expressed appreciation to General MacArthur." This photo of a subsequent public event shows the people's appreciation.

Emperor should be no more or no less than the legal protection accorded a citizen.

Sad and unpleasant task

Probably nothing during my administration of the Occupation gave me deeper concern than the obligation to act upon the judgment of the International Military Tribunal of the Far East. I had approved penalties adjudged against enemy field commanders or other military personnel who had permitted or committed atrocities against soldiers or civilians who had fallen under their custody during the war, but the principle of holding criminally responsible the political leaders of the vanquished in war was repugnant to me. I felt that to do so was to violate the most fundamental rules of criminal justice. I believed, and I so recommended, that any criminal responsibility attached to Japanese political leaders for the decision to wage war should be limited to an indictment for the attack on Pearl Harbor, since this act was effected without a prior declaration of war as required by international law and custom. I was then relieved of all responsibility having to do with the actual trial procedures before the International Military Tribunal, which started sitting in Tokyo January 19, 1946. The tribunal was composed of distinguished jurists from the Allied powers nominated by their respective governments. My obligations did not even include the selection of those to be tried. My only duties were to pass on the final judgments of the tribunal and to enforce the sentences.

By the terms of the Potsdam declaration, I was to see that "stern justice shall be meted out to all war criminals." We had no trouble finding the individuals who were accused. Within a few weeks we had imprisoned such diverse characters as 'Tokyo Rose' and Prime Minister Tojo. The number of such prisoners ran into the hundreds. We made a distinction between major and minor war criminals. 'Tokyo Rose' was considered a minor one. So were the many guards at the various prisoner camps who had mistreated our people. They were tried and appropriate punishment was imposed. There were only twenty-eight major war criminals. These were the people in political offices and other positions who actually were responsible for taking Japan to war. Of these, only twenty-five were brought to trial, the other three dying or going insane before entering the courtroom. All twenty-five of those who stood trial were found guilty, including Prime Minister Tojo.

I was besieged with requests for permits to allow press photographers to record the actual executions. I refused on the grounds that such a spectacle would outrage the sensibilities of the Japanese, and high-minded people everywhere. The Secretary of the Army was asked to override my decision, but I refused to allow him to interfere, because in this particular case I was acting as a representative of international powers, rather than as an officer of the United States Army. The uproar soon died away, but to reassure the people of the world that the executions had actually taken place, I invited the members of the occupation advisory group, the Allied Council, to attend as official witnesses. All accepted, although reluctantly.

I was pleasantly surprised at the attitude of the Japanese people during the period of trial. They seemed to be impressed both by the fairness of the procedures and by the lack of vindictiveness on the part of the prosecutors. The prisoners themselves and their families made it a point to write letters to me and to the tribunal after their conviction to express their thanks for our impartiality and justice. No perceptible ill will was generated in Japan as a result of the trials.

29. Gen. MacArthur accepts United Nations colors. After the invasion of South Korea by North Korea communists, President Truman directed Gen. MacArthur to send troops on Occupation duty into Korea to halt the aggression. Subsequently, the United Nations confirmed this emergency action by the U.S. and appointed the General as Commander in Chief of a United Nations' effort to turn back the communist forces. This is symbolized (above) during a ceremony on the roof of the Dai Ichi Building. Honor Guard members can be seen in the background. *(U.S. Army Photo)*

Korean War
The General's Time Runs Out

From the time of the outbreak of the Korean War, the General's attention shifted to that crisis as he followed the actions of the enemy and commanded a desperate holding action against overwhelming North Korean forces supported by the Russians. In time, he built his forces with the support of many nations of the free world under the auspices of the United Nations. He planned a masterful strategy to breakout from a small stronghold at the southern tip of the Korean peninsula and launched an invasion into the center of enemy held territory, throroughly routing them. In weeks, the North Korean army was in shambles as UN forces fought their way to the northern border at Manchuria. The war would have been over were it not for the intervention of the Chinese Red Army, which with overwhelming numbers, pushed the UN troops back to near the original north-south demarcation.

It was at this point where General MacArthur and the President of the United States, Harry S Truman, began to differ sharply on the way to conduct the offense against the Chinese. The General strongly urged the use of air power to break Chinese supply lines, which meant bombing into Manchuria. Truman was fearful this would ignite a more widespread war, whereas the General believed the Chinese were not inclined or capable of engaging in a large scale war.

MacArthur writes in his <u>Reminicenses</u> that he

believed if the U.S. had warned the Chinese about entering the war that it could have been terminated at the point where the North Korean Army was defeated. He also asserts that a leak of intelligence provided information to the Chinese leaders that they could enjoy their sanctuary in Manchuria without attack.

Later an official leaflet attributed to Chinese General Lin Piao states: "I would never have made an attack and risked my men and military reputation if I had not been assured that Washington would restrain General MacArthur from taking retaliatory measures against my lines of supply and communication."

There has been much written about the discord between the President and his military leader, but the consensus is that the General overstepped, or was about to overstep, his authority. Beyond the obvious there was a long festering dislike and distrust between these two men and rampant political overtones. None should challenge the authority of the President to take action to remove his general, but personal rancor played a part in the way the matter was handled.

On April 11, 1951, the President called a press conference to announce General MacArthur's relief from command. The announcement reached Tokyo on the afternoon of the 11, as radios broke the news. The General had just finished lunch and was preparing to visit the front in Korea. Colonel Huff, an aide, heard the broadcast and called the residential quarters at the embassy to relay the news to the General's wife. After the initial shock, the General said, "Jeanie, we're going home at last."

General MacArthur had been on overseas duty for over fifteen years, since 1935, without a respite. During the occupation, a period of almost six years in Japan, there was no time off, no family vacation. His job was his life. He worked tirelessly, long hours every day, seven days a week. All of this by a man who was then in his seventies!

Sayonara

The Japanese Diet passed a resolution of tribute and thanks. The Emperor made a farewell call of sorrow. Prime Minister Yoshida broadcast to the nation saying: "The accomplishments of General MacArthur in the interest of our country are one of the marvels of history. It is he who has salvaged our nation from post-surrender confusion and prostration, and steered the country on the road of recovery and reconstruction. It is he who has firmly planted democracy in all segments of our society. It is he who has paved the way for a peace settlement. No wonder he is looked upon by all our people with the profoundest veneration and affection. I have no words to convey the regret of our nation to see him leave."

And in a personal note to me Yoshida wrote: "Words fail me to tell you how shocked and how grieved I am at your precipitous departure from our shores. In this personal note it would be super-fluous of me to duplicate the resolutions and testimonials of appreciation and thanks which are being sent to you from both Houses of the Diet and many other quarters, and which constitute a spontaneous tribute of the nation to the monumental task you have accomplished as Supreme Commander for the Allied Powers in rebuilding and revitalizing our country. All Japanese from the Emperor to the man on the street regret your going."

I received letters from Natokesato, the president of the House of Councillors: "The sudden news was so shocking to me that I have not yet recovered from its effects. The feeling of a great regret together with an irrevocable loss and bewilderment is shared by the people of entire Japan. They sorrow from the bottom of their hearts to have to part with the great leader whom they have loved and trusted. Since my appointment as the President of the House of Councillors, your wise counsel gave me courage and

30. Japanese mourn the General's departure. Millions of Japanese lined the roadways to say sayonara to the man who had lifted them out of their destitute state at the end of the war and helped them to establish a democratic government to their everlasting benefit. President Truman rightfully recalled the General because of policy differences, but the manner in which it was done was unbefitting a person who had done so much for his country.

(U.S. Army Photo)

now the prospect of your departure saddens me profoundly."

Kotaro Tanaka, Chief Justice of the Japan Supreme Court wrote: "It is with the deepest regret that I learned of the sudden departure of Your Excellency, who has gained the everlasting respect and admiration of the Japanese people by your great leadership in the reconstruction and democratization of Japan. The fruit of the great achievements of Your Excellency, rarely seen in the annals of history, are ready to be crowned with the signing of the Peace Treaty. I am sure that you must feel great satisfaction in the healthy progress of a peaceful and democratic Japan, established by the ideals of your noble and farsighted policies based on your firm religious faith. On your departure, I wish to express my deepest sorrow and my hearty gratitude on behalf of the Supreme Court, and the entire judicial branch of the Japanese Government, for your great material and spiritual aid and advice, especially the benevolent advice and assistance given the Japanese Courts, and also the precious achievements left by Your Excellency."

The two leading papers, the Asahi Shimbum and the Mainichi Shimbum, had spoken: "The removal is a great disappointment to the Japanese, especially when the peace settlement is so near. We feel as if we had lost a kind and loving father. His recall is the greatest shock since the end of the war. He dealt with the Japanese people not as a conqueror but as a great reformer. He was a noble political missionary. What he gave us was not material aid and democratic reform alone — but a new way of life, the freedom and dignity of the individual. We shall continue to love and trust him as one who best understood Japan's position. We wanted his further help in nurturing our green democracy to fruition. We wanted his leadership at least until a signed peace treaty had given us a sendoff into the world community."

(End of the General's Reminiscences in direct context)

31. Japanese officials say sayonara. Premier Shigeru Yoshida with his daughter, to his left, and Joji Hayashi, President of the Japanese House of Representative, to his right, were among thousands of Japanese and Americans hastily gathered to say farewell to Gen. MacArthur and his family at Haneda Airport. Premier Yoshida and Gen. MacArthur had worked together effectively. The General felt that Yoshida was sympathetic to SCAP policies, yet a fair advocate for the Japanese people. However, when the situation was contentious, Yoshida was reputably the only Japanese politician who dared to stand up to the General and his SCAP policy makers. *(U.S. Army Photo)*

32. Emperor makes amends. Emperor Hirohito made a commitment to meet as many of the Japanese as possible, face-to-face, to express his concern and sympathy for the hardships brought about by the war. Between 1945 and 1950, he literally covered Japan, going from one prefecture to the next to meet the people. The photo above shows the Emperor (tipping hat) in November, 1946, during a visit to Ibaragi Prefecture. American Military Police provided security for the Emperor.

V

JAPAN REJOINS THE WORLD COMMUNITY OF FREE AND INDEPENDENT NATIONS

From the outset General MacArthur was very clear that the purpose of his mission, once the Japanese war machine and related matters were disposed of, was to accomplish a democratic social and political restructuring which would make Japan a nation of self-governing people. After five years under his direction, influence, and tutoring, the General believed they achieved these objectives. He was proud to make the following statement to the Japanese people on the occasion of the fifth anniversary of VJ Day:

"Five years have passed since the nations of the world entered into solemn covenants designed to restore and preserve the peace. All men then looked forward with new hope and a new resolve to achieve a relationship based upon a mutuality of purpose, a mutuality of understanding, and a mutuality of dedication to higher human and spiritual ideals. Hope found its genesis in the determination enunciated by the major powers that irresponsible militarism, the scourge of mankind since the beginning of time, be driven from the world.

"This hope has not materialized. While militarism in Japan, largely through the self-dedicated efforts of the Japanese people themselves, has been banished and no longer

135

33. Working out the treaty. Gen. MacArthur accompanies U.S. Secretary of State John Foster Dulles to the Haneda Airport after discussions of details of the U.S.- Japan Peace Treaty. Although the General was residing in the States at the time the treaty was signed in San Francisco in 1951, he was snubbed for political reasons and not invited to the signing.

exists even as a debatable concept, elsewhere imperialistic militarism, marching under different banners but unified direction, is leaving in its wake the stark tragedy of human and spiritual wreckage. Many peoples have fallen under its savage and merciless assaults and fear of conquest and enslavement grips much of the earth.

"In the universal atmosphere of doubt and uncertainty generated by the clash of opposing forces — good and evil — the Japanese people with calmness and resolution have written a record of political reorientation, economic reconstruction and social progress which attests to Japan's unconditional qualification to resume membership in good standing in the family of free nations. From the ashes left in war's wake there has arisen in Japan an edifice dedicated to the primacy of individual liberty and personal dignity, and in the ensuing process there has been created a truly representative government committed to the advance of political morality, freedom of economic enterprise, and social justice. Thus oriented, Japan may be counted upon to wield a profound influence over the course of events in Asia.

"The basic objectives of Occupation have been achieved. Politically, economically, and socially, Japan at peace will not fail the universal trust."

For many months prior to this statement, the General had advised the U.S. State Department of the progress which could lead to the end of the Occupation and a peace treaty that would make Japan an independent nation. At first many in Washington were skeptical about withdrawing control and allowing Japan to once again join the world community of free nations. However, with MacArthur's guidance and dedicated efforts of the Japanese people and their political leaders and statesmen, confidence grew. On September 8, 1950, Gen. MacArthur received the following communication from the State Department:

"We have been making progress on the Japanese Peace Treaty matter and now finally the State and Defense Departments are in agreement to proceed, and on the general goals to be sought. I expect that we shall take the occasion of the forthcoming New York meetings of the Foreign Ministers and of the delegates at the United Nations Assembly to feel out informally the views of some of our friendly allies as to future procedure. Our present conclusions here coincide with the views which you put forward to Secretary Johnson and to me and I feel that your position created the bridge over which we can now make constructive progress. In view of the tendency of the United Nations Assembly, probably no major steps, certainly of a formal nature, can be taken for two or three months yet. But some useful preliminary work can perhaps be done so that the time will not really be lost. I hope that someone from the Department will shortly again be in Tokyo to talk over future steps with you. With my best wishes and admiration for the magnificent way in which you are carrying your new responsibilities, I am

Faithfully yours, John Foster Dulles"

Work on the treaty, under the auspices of the State Department, was pursued with vigor and determination to bring it to a conclusion during the term of the Truman Administration. Mr. Dulles and his staff were on a tight schedule, working on a document that would not only satisfy Japan and the United States but also its major allies. Early the next year, a delegation from the State Department set out for Tokyo to seek a final meeting of the minds and a resolution of details. The General wrote the following:

"A mission headed by Ambassador John Foster Dulles came to Tokyo on January 22, to work out the final details of the peace treaty with Japan. They stayed until February 9th, and, with the complete cooperation of the Japanese, appeared to make firm progress. I worked hand-in-hand with Dulles, continually stressing the fact that Japan deserved the treaty and that its realization would restore a defeated people to their place among nations of the world. The treaty itself would show the people of Asia that the United States was not a conqueror but a friend.

"Not too long afterward, a peace treaty was signed in San Francisco amid great pomp and ceremony. I was not invited to attend. Perhaps someone just forgot to remember."

One can feel the disappointment and sadness in the General's last remark. He was being snubbed by an administration in Washington which was quick to take the credit for much of what the General had accomplished. He did not strike back at his detractors, however, because he knew the Japanese people appreciated and understood his role and that history would record his deeds.

And the Japanese people did display their appreciation and warmth for the General on the day of his departure, April 16, 1951. Two million saddened and distraught Japanese lined the route from the American Embassy to the airfield at Atsugi, where the General would forever leave Japanese soil. Later the General was honored with the Grand Cordon of the Order of the Rising Sun with Paulonia Flowers, one of the highest awards of the nation which was reserved for monarchs and heads of government. The text of the citation is worthy of remembrance.

"This high decoration for distinguished service is awarded you in recognition especially of your great contribution to the postwar reconstruction of Japan and to the development of the immense reservoir of good will that exists between our two nations today. Your role as Supreme Commander of Allied Powers in Japan will certainly go down in history as the greatest of all examples of enlightened occupation administration; and it will for all time be remembered with devoted gratitude by the Japanese people. In the trying days after the war you instilled hope and a sense of direction into the Japanese people. You helped them regain their self-respect and rebuild their economic life. Under your leadership, Japan became a nation of free men, thereby laying the basis for her membership in the free world. Both the Japanese Government and the Japanese people are entering the second century of their relations with the United States with the conviction that their future lies with the nations of the free world, and particularly in friendship and cooperation with the United States."

This great and deserved tribute to the General demonstrated the warmth and sincerity of the Japanese people as they recognized the accomplishments of his dedicated service.

Upon the General's return to the United States, he made an historic address to a joint session of Congress in which he reviewed his military career and proudly said the following about the Japanese people with whom he had spent the past six years:

"The Japanese people since the war have undergone the greatest reformation recorded in modern history. With a commendable will, eagerness to learn, and marked capacity to understand, they have, from the ashes left in war's wake, erected in Japan an edifice dedicated to the primacy of individual liberty and personal dignity, and in the ensuing process there has been created a truly representative government committed to the advance of political morality, freedom of economic enterprise, and social justice. Politically, economically and socially, Japan is now abreast of many free nations of the earth and will not again fail the universal trust. That it may be counted upon to wield a profoundly beneficial influence over the course of events in Asia is attested by the magnificent manner in which the Japanese people have met the recent challenge of war, unrest and confusion surrounding them from the outside, and checked Communism within their own frontiers without the slightest slackening in their forward progress. I sent all four of our occupation divisions to the Korean battlefront without the slightest qualms as to the effect of the resulting power vacuum upon Japan. The results fully justified my faith. I know of no nation more secure, orderly and industrious — nor in which higher hopes can be entertained for future constructive service in the advance of the human race."

34. Gen. MacArthur's Honor Guard. The Honor Guard Company is shown entering the South Portal of the Imperial Palace grounds. These elite troops frequently marched on review, especially for visiting dignitaries, and in observance of holidays. Japanese were much in awe of the smartly dressed and well-drilled troops of the Honor Guard. Half of the company was billeted at the Japanese Finance Ministry building, a few blocks from the palace grounds, the other half was billeted at the American Embassy. Their primary duty stations were the Dai Ichi Building, headquarters of GHQ and the General's official office, and the American Embassy where the General lived with family and staff.

VII
TWELVE YEAR OLDS

A weakness of lesser mortals is a pre-disposition to try to reduce people of great stature down to a more earthy level. Perhaps this is a way of coping with feelings of inadequacy. Some will denigrate the reputation, image or legacy of persons of exalted stature by a willingness to accept anything derogatory about the personage, with little objective scrutiny or interest in putting the criticism into proper perspective. This seems to be what happened in the case of General MacArthur's remark, in testimony to the U.S. Congress, about Japanese being like twelve-year-olds.

Up until this time General MacArthur was held in the highest regard by the Japanese people, but after a few news stories, and either poor or slanted reporting of his remark, the General's public image came tumbling down. It is sad to think how this must have hurt his feelings, as he was well aware of what was going on in Japan, but he was a man content in his convictions and his respect for the Japanese people. He would not plead for their understanding.

Since this unfortunate incident, much has been written on the subject and the facts are available to anyone who wishes to examine them. A thorough and insightful study has been done by a Japanese writer, Taga Toshiyuki, manager of domestic information in the Ministry of Foreign Affairs.[7] The following paragraphs are from the Toshiyuki report.

At the Senate Hearings on Military and Diplomatic Affairs, which began on May 5, 1951, MacArthur, in replying to Committee member Long's questions, remarked that when he looked back at human history he could see that there has never been a successful occupation, and that the one exception was that of Julius Caesar. Further, he went on,

---

[7]Taga Toshiyuki, <u>Bungei Shunju</u>, September, 1993, pp 369-375

the occupation of Japan was like the case of Julius Caesar,

being a successful example of an occupation. The Japanese are so deeply impressed that the American occupation soldiers did not plunder or exploit them that they have come to respect the Americans. The Japanese have now tasted freedom. Freedom not merely as rhetoric. They now know true freedom through their experience of it. There is no people who have gladly abandoned freedom on their own once they have tasted it.

Committee member Long responded to these comments of MacArthur with, "After World War I, the Germans should have tasted freedom, even if only temporarily." MacArthur until this comment had talked on about what a good thing the Japanese occupation had been. There is no doubt that

---

In response to Chairman Long's statement, the General said, "If Anglo Saxons have reached the prime of life at 45 in terms of science, art, culture and other areas of development, then the Germans are at about the same level. But the Japanese are still students, twelve-year-old adolescents. The Germans were aware that they were transgressing modern ethics and international morality. It is not a fact that they were unaware of the international situation, and the mistake they made is somewhat different in content than that committed by the Japanese."

---

this unexpected question was like a bolt from the blue. MacArthur was taken aback.

(Toshiyuki's report continues) I'm sure he must have felt in his heart that he couldn't bear to have his own occupation policies in Japan so confused with Germany that his policies were not appraised properly. He must have felt there was a necessity to emphasize strongly the differences with Germany.

Unfortunately, this statement has been taken out of its actual context and has taken on a life of its own. It has become firmly entrenched among the Japanese people mainly as an expression of contempt of the Japanese. The movement at the time to make MacArthur a 'permanent guest,' as well as that to build a General MacArthur Memorial Hall, a movement sponsored by Prince Chichiibu, the Princess, the head Diet librarian Kanemori, the Supreme Court Justice Tanaka, the Mainichi Newspaper head Honda, and the Asahi Newspaper head Hasebe and other (fourteen in all) dignified gentlemen, all came to naught.

The fact that MacArthur's "twelve-year-old" statement had taken on a meaning different from what he had originally intended was also pointed out by former Prime Minister Shigeru Yoshida in Volume I of his <u>Remembering Ten Years</u>, written back in 1957. This revelation also seems to have been nearly completely forgotten today. Yoshida says:

When the General was relieved of his duties, returned to the United States and gave his speech to the Senate (this was actually in a committee hearing), his words, 'Japanese are twelve-year-olds' was reported in the press, and misunderstood somehow to mean that the General was denigrating Japanese intelligence. In some circles it was even taken to be self-scorn. This is an extreme simplification and incomplete representation on the part of the right-wing press. When you read the details of the General's speech, it had the meaning, 'Japanese are still young when it comes to freedom and democratic government,' and is emphasizing that, 'because they have a unique, ancient culture and superior qualities, there are high hopes of future Japanese development to be made even on top of a system of civilization that is western in mode.' His real intent is no different from the high regard and expectations he always held for the Japanese."

End of Toshiyuki's report

The irony of the General's statement of the Japanese being like twelve-year-olds is that some Japanese proved him more literally correct by acting like twelve-year-olds. How like a child to smart from a misunderstood remark and rebel, rather than to seek its truth and learn from it. Whether these Japanese have grown substantially since may be shown by their willingness to re-examine the legacy of General MacArthur and give it its rightful place in the annals of Japanese history.

VI
HONOR GUARD MISSION

In early May, 1945, an order went out to all combat divisions in the Pacific Command to select ten of their best soldiers for assignment at general headquarters at Manila. These men were to form a guard of honor for General MacArthur and other general officers and visiting dignitaries. The selection criteria for these men was exceptionally high. Candidates must have a score of 110 or better on the Army General Classification Test, must have an excellent service record as a combat soldier, be of good physique and over five feet ten inches tall. Exceptional soldiers came from Moresby, Moratai, Leyte and Luzon. These two hundred men then assembled, who had fought the Japanese on the beaches, in the jungles, and in the mountains, formed the Honor Guard, representing all the fighting men of the Southwest Pacific Area. This unit was probably the sharpest, most elite unit formed during World War II.

The Honor Guard Company, among the first troops to enter Japan, took over duties of guarding General MacArthur, his family and staff. This included both the American Embassy, where the MacArthur family and many staff were in residence, and the Dai Ichi Building, GHQ headquarters, where the General and his staff worked. Anyone visiting those places during the Occupation could not fail to notice the presence and outstanding appearance of the Honor Guard. They served General MacArthur well and faithfully during those years, without incident or any threat to those they were charged to protect. Their final salute to the General at Atsugi, April 16, 1951, was a time of sadness. Many guardsmen who had remained in the service to serve the General resigned after his departure and returned to the States.

About thirty years later, a former guardsman, Bob Marko of Indiana, was contacted by an old buddy, Henry Doyel of California, and their discussions eventually led to the forming of The General MacArthur Honor Guard Association. They attempted to locate all former members of the Honor Guard who served under General MacArthur. Over the years, with thousands of letters and phone calls,

35. Gen. MacArthur statue at Atsugi, Japan. Japanese businessman Kenkichi Takahashi, of Kanagawa, donated the statue of Gen. MacArthur at the Atsugi Airbase, where the General first landed with American troops August 30, 1945. This base is now shared by U.S. Naval and Japan Self Defense Force fighter aircraft. Mr. Takahashi's generosity made this outstanding memorial possible. It was his way, on behalf of the Japanese people, to show gratitude for the General's contributions to the welfare of the Japanese people. Standing in front of the statue are Mr. & Mrs. John Schuelke. John is a former Honor Guard. He married his lovely wife Fumiko in 1956.

they were remarkably successful in locating, or recording the demise of, the majority of those who served, about 1200 members. The Association has held bi-annual reunions since 1985, and in 1987 a contingent went on to Tokyo after their reunion in San Francisco.

Today members of the Honor Guard are in their very late sixties, with most in their seventies or older. We are at the stage in life when we can see the events of the past in better perspective and have come to appreciate the greatness of our country and the outstanding contributions made by General MacArthur. Of course, we are especially devoted to the General, because of our service connection, but many Americans, knowing as we do of his greatness, would feel the same way. Yet, recent generations are either unfamiliar with their heritage or indifferent about it. Our mission now goes beyond recalling the times past for our own benefit as we bring to the public, in the States and in Japan, the story of General MacArthur and the Occupation of Japan.

As at our origin, when we were selected to represented a large body of the military in the Pacific, we now seek to carry on that role by recognizing all military personnel who served well and faithfully during the Occupation of Japan. We ask them to join us, in body or in spirit, as we prepare for a commemorative celebration in Japan in the year 2001 to mark the 50th anniversary of General MacArthur's departure and honor all who served during the Occupation.

A list of former Honor Guard members, according to the latest records of the Association, is given in the Appendix. Should anyone be interested in contacting members, or the Association, he may write to the publisher, The Sektor Company, Post Office Box 501005, San Diego, CA 92150.

GENERAL DOUGLAS MacARTHUR FOUNDATION
MacARTHUR SQUARE — NORFOLK, VIRGINIA 23510

Dear Mr. Marko

I heard that the reunion of the Ho
I cannot let the day pass without
was made up of outstanding men.
enough for your dedication to "m
services you performed for me per

I wish I could be with you on thi
you.

Jean MacArthur

Mrs. Douglas MacArthur

36. Mrs. Douglas MacArthur and the Honor Guard. The gracious Mrs. Douglas MacArthur, celebrated her 101st birthday on December 28, 1999, and passed away just as this book was going to press, on January 10, 2000. She is held in the highest esteem by members of the Honor Guard. Their Association, which holds reunions every two years, sent an invitation to Mrs. MacArthur on each occasion. One of her replies is shown above, with a recent picture. The message reads:

"I heard the Honor Guard reunion is taking place in August this year. I cannot let the day pass without sending you my best wishes. The Honor Guard was made up of outstanding men. Many of you I knew personally. I can't say enough for your dedication to 'my general' and for all the little favors and services you performed for me personally. I wish I could be with you on this festive occasion and reminisce with each of you.

Jean MacArthur"

VIII

HOW WAS
THIS
ALL POSSIBLE?

Looking at the Occupation in its entirety after nearly fifty years, observing that so much of great consequence was accomplished in a relatively short period of time, it is fair to ask, "How was this all possible?" This book makes the case for the personal efforts of General MacArthur and the policies, largely decided by the Americans. It also points out the significant role of the Emperor, Japanese leaders, and particularly the willingness of the Japanese people. But, "How so?"

Ruth Benedict, the eminent American anthropologist, who unmasked the soul of the Japanese in her outstanding work, The Chrysanthemum and the Sword[8] can give us the benefit of her insight. The gist of this is, the Japanese people possessed a remarkable attitude as a result of their cultural heritage which made the challenge attainable. The following paragraphs are from her book, which was written at the time of the Occupation.

> Japan's real strength which she can use in remaking herself into a peaceful nation lies in her ability to say of a course of action, "That failed," and then to throw her energies into other channels. The Japanese have an ethic of alternatives. They tried to achieve their "proper place" in the war, and they lost. That course, now, they can discard, because their whole training has conditioned them to possible changes of direction. Nations with a more absolutist

---

[8]Ruth Benedict, The Chrysanthemum and the Sword, Meridian Books, Cleveland and New York, 1946. pp.304 - 310

ethic must convince themselves that they are fighting for principles. When they surrender to the victors, they say, "Right was lost when we were defeated," and their self-respect demands that they work to make this "right" win the next time. Or they can beat their breasts and confess their guilt. The Japanese need do neither.

The Westerner observes this shift in what he regards as principles and suspects it. It is, however, an integral part of the conduct of life in Japan, whether in personal or international relations.

The Japanese sees that he has made an "error" in embarking on a course of action which does not achieve its goal. When it fails, he discards it as a lost cause, for he is not conditioned to pursue lost causes. 'It is no use,' he says, 'biting one's navel.' Militarism was in the nineteen-thirties the accepted means by which they thought to gain the admiration of the world — an admiration to be based on their armed might — and they accepted all the sacrifices such a program required. On August 14, 1945, the Emperor, the sanctioned voice of Japan, told them that they had lost. They accepted all that such a fact implied. It meant the presence of American troops, so they welcomed them. It meant failure of their dynastic enterprise, so they were willing to consider a Constitution which outlawed war.

American administration of Japan under General MacArthur has accepted this Japanese ability to sail a new course. It has not impeded that course by insisting on using techniques of humiliation. It would have been culturally acceptable according to Western ethics if we had done so. For it is a tenet of Occidental ethics that humiliation and punishment are socially effective means to bring about a wrongdoer's conviction of sin. Such an admission of sin is then a first step in his rehabilitation. The Japanese, as we have seen, state the issue in another way. Their ethic makes a man responsible for all the implications of his acts, and the natural consequences of an error should convince him of its undesirability. These natural consequences may even be defeat in an all-out war. But these are not situations that the Japanese must resent as humiliating. In the Japanese lexicon, a person or nation humiliates another by detraction, ridicule, contempt, belittling, and insisting on symbols of dishonor. When the Japanese believe themselves humiliated, revenge is a virtue. No matter how strongly Western ethics condemn such a tenet, the effectiveness of American occupation of Japan depends on American self-restraint on this point. For the Japanese separate ridicule, which they terribly resent, from 'natural consequences,' which according to the terms of their surrender include such things as demilitarization and even Spartan imposition of indemnities.

The final victory of the United States again changed the situation for Japan. Their ultimate defeat brought about, as is usual in Japanese life, the abandonment of the course they had been pursuing. The peculiar ethic of the Japanese allowed them to wipe the slate clean. United States' policy and General MacArthur's administration have avoided writing fresh symbols of humiliation upon that washed slate, and have held simply to insisting on those things which in Japanese eyes are 'natural consequences' of defeat. It has worked.

The retention of the Emperor has been of great impor-
tance. It has been handled well. It was the Emperor who
called first on MacArthur, not MacArthur who called
upon him, and this was an object lesson to the Japanese
the force of which it is hard for Westerners to appreciate.
It is said that when it was suggested to the Emperor that
he disavow his divinity, he protested that it would be a personal embarrassment to strip himself of something he did
not have. The Japanese, he said truthfully, did not consider him a god in the Western sense. MacArthur's
Headquarters, however, urged upon him that the
Occidental idea of his claim to divinity was bad for
Japan's international repute, and the Emperor agreed to
accept the embarrassment the disavowal would cost him.
He spoke on New Year's Day, and asked to have all comments on his message translated for him from the world
press. When he read them, he sent a message to General
MacArthur's Headquarters saying that he was satisfied.
Foreigners had obviously not understood before, and he
was glad he had spoken.

The Japanese have taken the first great step toward
social change by identifying aggressive warfare as an
'error' and a lost cause. They hope to buy their passage
back to a respected place among peaceful nations.

This concludes the brilliant analysis by Ruth Benedict

Americans in the Occupation learned much about the Japanese
spirit and industrious habits. Though many of us, having grown up
during the Great Depression, had experienced the difficulties of
'scraping by,' the Japanese seemed to take dealing with adversity to
a higher place. There was something special about how they got by
with so little, yet maintained a cheerful and positive attitude. They

were ubiquitous among Occupation forces, doing the most menial jobs with dignity and cheerfulness. They had a more developed sense of how to deliver "service" with their jobs, and seemed sincere in their desire to please. Their attitude and diligent work ethics earned our respect.

In contrast, years later the author had an opportunity to observe the work ethic of another Asian people, the Chinese in Shanghai, in the mid-eighties. Their demeanor was generally pleasant toward foreigners, but their work habits in some situations reflected an attitude of disinterest or worse. In the case below, it may have been more a reaction to the Communist system in which they lived, than personal inclinations.

I visited the largest department store in Shanghai, a government-owned enterprise. The store was shabby and the goods, by Western standards, were mostly of low quality, but that much was predictable. What was most surprising was the lack of good housekeeping and cleanliness. Aisles were cluttered with empty boxes and debris, and the stairways between floors were little more than rubbish heaps. When I asked my guide why there was such a mess, she told me frankly, "Everyone gets the same pay whether they stand behind the counter or do the dirty cleaning; no one wants to do the cleaning and what is done is not very good." A lesson in democracy — free enterprise creates opportunities, not just jobs, and the pursuit of opportunities can be accomplished with high purpose and dignity.

Free enterprise also fosters ingenuity, the ability to turn what is available into something of value to create wealth. We had a saying, "If you throw away a beer can, the next day you will see it as part of a toy being sold on the Ginza." This was literally true as many clever Japanese took whatever they had by way of skills and available materials to provide services or goods to sell to the Americans. This has become the cornerstone of their economy. Who could have suspected then, that Japan within twenty-five years would completely overtake the United States in production of consumer entertainment goods, have a burgeoning GNP and positive balance of payments?

Viva democracy and free enterprise!

IX
AFTERTHOUGHTS

The purpose of this book is to tell a story, a true story based on historical events, with the intent to present a positive portrayal of an outstanding chapter in the life of General Douglas A. MacArthur, and to show its great impact on the Japanese people and nation. This is done in the hope that younger generations of Japanese will know the Gaijin Shojun and accord him a high place in Japanese history.

Is it the whole story? Certainly not. It focuses on the General's role, mostly his view of it, but it is supported by library shelves of evidence. Is there another side to the story? Yes, there is always another side and this is no exception. No events, policies, or programs serve only the intended ends. The framers do not do things perfectly and positions must be compromised to some extent to obtain support from other quarters. Were all members of GHQ high-minded and well-intentioned? There were certainly some who did not always adhere to the ideals and objectives of the General and those of an independent persuasion, but that is to be expected in any organization. It is an unhealthy environment if some cannot question and challenge the prevailing wisdom; opposing opinion is needed to reach the best solutions. However, it is also true that some policies were flawed, unfair, and poorly conceived as well.

But for whatever criticism can be raised, there is an overwhelming counter-argument. The General believed in the Japanese people and so designed, construed, and promulgated the reconstruction of Japan that the people could judge and correct any flaws that the Occupation policies might induce. His faith in the Japanese people on occasion even exceeded that of the Japanese themselves. Prime Minister Yoshida tells this story:

"In conversation with the General he mentioned his admiration of exceptional military leaders of the Russo-Japanese War era, Admiral Togo and General Nogi (whom he had met on a goodwill visit to Japan many years earlier). I once pointed out to him that men like Togo and Nogi were exceptional types such as no longer existed in the Japan of today, but he refused to be convinced, replying that it was strange that I, as a Japanese, should seek to denigrate my own people and adding that, if one considered the farmers working in the fields from early morning until late at night — not only men but also women and young girls — and further, remembered the achievements of the Japanese in various fields of scientific research, it was clear that as a race they were inferior to none in the world."[9]

In business it is widely recognized that the mark of a great manager is the subsequent greatness of the people he leads. And so it is today that the greatness of the Japanese people is, in some way, a measure of the greatness of General MacArthur, the Gaijin Shogun, stepfather of modern Japan.

---

[9] Shigeru Yoshida, The Yoshida Memoirs, Houghton Mifflin Co., Boston, 1963, pp. 48-49

Rather than have an American conclude this book with a statement about the success of the Occupation, again we turn to the heartfelt remarks of Prime Minister Shigeru Yoshida.

"Japan's occupation of various Asian countries became an object of hatred and loathing among the peoples of the occupied countries, and there are none to dispute that fact. The Americans came into our country as our enemies, but after an occupation lasting little less than seven years, an understanding grew up between the two peoples which is remarkable in the history of the modern world.

Criticism of Americans is a right accorded even to Americans. But in the enumeration of their faults we cannot include the Occupation of Japan."[10]

The end

---

[10] Ibid, Yoshida, page 60

37. Douglas MacArthur Memorial, Norfolk, VA.
'Duty, Honor, Country'

GEN. MACARTHUR
MEMORIAL - NORFOLK, VA

Beautifully landscaped MacArthur Square in downtown Norfolk, Virginia, is the site of the four buildings that comprise the General Douglas MacArthur Memorial.

The Memorial's theater contains several special exhibit galleries and continuously shows a twenty-four minute film on the life and times of General of the Army Douglas MacArthur, one of the most colorful and controversial men in American history. The Jean MacArthur Research Center (named after the General's wife) houses the library and archives, an education wing, and the administrative offices for the MacArthur Memorial and the General Douglas MacArthur Foundation. The gift shop displays General MacArthur's 1950 Chrysler Imperial limousine which he used from 1950 to the end of his life.

The museum proper is housed in Norfolk's stately nineteenth century City Hall. The monumental rotunda is the General's final resting place where he lies surrounded by inscriptions, banners, and flags heralding his long and glorious career. Nine separate galleries arranged in two levels circle the rotunda and portray the principal periods of the General's life.

A visit to the MacArthur Memorial provides a unique glimpse into the 20th century and can renew your faith in those American values of Duty-Honor-Country, values which motivated Douglas MacArthur as he served our nation through some of its greatest crises and finest hours.

Website http//sites.communitylink.org/mac/

38. Official Commemoration Seal. Cherry blossoms on the left and dogwood blossoms on the right are symbolic of Japan and America.

HONOR GUARD
ROLL CALL

The following is a list of members of the Gen. MacArthur Honor Guard Association, as of 1999. All members were assigned to the Honor Guard between May 4, 1944 and April 16, 1951. We regret there is not a list of all who served or of those who are now deceased. Should a reader wish to contact any person listed below, he may write to: Gen. MacArthur Honor Guard Assoc., Post Office Box 501005, San Diego, CA 92150, and his request will be forwarded to the person.

Alaska

Boston, Billy F. - *Anchorage*

Alabama

Hall, David - *Dothan*
Krotchko, Gene G. - *Huntsville*

Arkansas

Christensen, Harry - *Rose Bud*
Clark, John M. - *Rogers*
Conway, Thomas F.- *Arkadelphia*
Dodd, Brown E. - *Searcy*
Fair, Paul R. - *Little Rock*
McGinnis, Claude P. - *Bella Vista*
Talburt, Rex D. - *Harrison*
Tidwell, Thomas E. - *Pine Bluff*
Walters, Otha L. - *Hot Springs*

Arizona

Antil, James A. - *Sun City West*
Avidan, Irwin - *Sun City West*
Babson, Robert F. - *Rimrock*
Branch, Dave - *Prescott*
Hickerson, Carl W. - *Scottsdale*
Hought, Robert L. - *Mesa*
Miller, Robert L. - *Mesa*
Porter, Raymond R. - *Fountain Hills*

Poteete, Delmar A. - *Mesa*
Simpson, Kenneth W. - *Tuscon*
Speakman, Roland H. - *Sedona*
Wheeler Sr., Harrison L. - *Prescott*

California

Baerresen, Richard - *Danville*
Balatti, Walter - *Concord*
Barouh, Albert - *Beverly Hills*
Bringham, Wm. - *Mission Viejo*
Butterfield,Ralph S. - *Walnut Creek*
Cabot, Jack W. - *Santa Barbara*
Cameron, Thomas J. - *Hawthorne*
Carmichael, Franklin - *Bakersfield*
Clarke, Robert N. - *Magalia*
Clifton, L. H. - *Palm Desert*
Cochrell, Cary M. - *Los Gatos*
Crawford, Clyde B. - *Paradise*
Cummings, Kenneth O. - *Andersen*
Dahlquist, George - *Thousand Palms*
Davies, Clyde - *San Diego*
Dawson, Martin I. - *Montgomery Creek*
Day, Homer E. - *Salinas*
De Moulin, John H. - *Concord*
DeWet, Charles W. - *Claremont*

Dixon, Arnold - *Chowchilla*
Doyel, Henry A. - *Vallejo*
DuPass, Redford J. - *Sacramento*
Durnin, John E. - *Santa Maria*
Fish, Niton D. - *Red Bluff*
Fish, Robert C. - *Solana Beach*
Fishel, Frank R. - *San Clemente*
Franks, Leslie - *Bakersfield*
Gamache, Rene J. - *Sylmar*
Gilkey, Estol B. - *McKinleyville*
Gray, Joe C. - *Santa Clara*
Hanes, Charlie F. - *Alameda*
Hanner, John, *Highland*
Hengstler, David E. - *Calabasas*
Ingerson, David L. - *Long Beach*
Jess, James F. - *Palm Springs*
Johnson, Donald R. - *Concord*
Johnson, Robert A. - *San Pedro*
Kibbey, Gerald - *San Diego*
Klecker, John W. - *Rancho Palos Verdes*
Kulas, Edward M. - *San Francisco*
Lehman, Robert - *Elk Grove*
Lenius, John E. - *Salinas*
L'eureux, Richard - *Huntington Beach*
L'Heureux, Homer A. - *San Diego*
Lucas, Sydney A. - *Corona Del Mar*
McLaughlin, Wilbur A. - *San Francisco*
Medley, Walter S. - *Greenville*
Michels, Francis J. - *Granada Hills*
Moshantz, Eugune H. - *Palm Desert*
Murray, John S. - *Carlsbad*
Nansel, Leon - *Apple Valley*
Opffer, Sebastian - *Santa Monica*
Phippen, Robert - *Chico*

Pia, Hugo - *Salinas*
Rains, Lawrence W. - *Newport Beach*
Reed, Francis F. - *La Palma*
Rehse, Vernon L. - *Orland*
Revolinksy, Philip A. - *Oroville*
Roth, Rex - *Long Beach*
Rudolph, Arthur D. - *Oceanside*
Rutherford, Harold E. - *Sacramento*
Schwickrath, John - *San Carlos*
Smith, George R. - *Concord*
Smith, Norman D. - *Ridgecrest*
Smythe, Vernon B. - *Huntington Beach*
Steed, George W. - *San Diego*
Stringham, Robert P. - *Tulare*
Underwood, Bob E. - *Vacaville*
Valley, David J. - *San Diego*
Vilkin , Max - *Sherman Oaks*
Vitrano, John - *Millbrae*
Wills, Howard - *Costa Mesa*
Wilson , Donald L. - *Fortuna*
Wollam, Miles E. - *La Canada*
Wray, Charles E. - *Whittier*
Zeager, James M. - *Oakland*

Colorado

Birdwell, Wilburn T. - *Colorado Springs*
Bond, Howard D. - *Lafayette*
Joy, Rollie L. - *Aurora*
Righter, Aubrey W. - *Colorado Springs*
Rodriquez, Manuel - *Commerce City*
Steele, George - *Grand Junction*
Walter, Frederick M. - *Englewood*

Connecticut

Discola, James W. - *East Haddam*

APPENDIX B: HONOR GUARD ROLL CALL

Hoffman, Karl E. - *New Fairfield*
Johanson, Lawrence T. - *Plainville*
Leckowicz, Walter J. - *Newington*
Lusk, Donald H. - *Voluntown*
Mann, Harry C. - *Plainfield*
Morris Sr., John W. - *Ridgefield*
Orlomoski, Alton L. - *Canterbury*
Sherwood, Charles - *New Haven*

District of Columbia

McCarthy, Thomas J. - *Washington*

Delaware

Nehrbas, Robert S. - *Milton*
Siltzer Sr., George S. - *Wilmington*

Florida

Auvil, William T. - *Tampa*
Bandy, Victor E. - *Naples*
Bechtel , Rodney E. - *Sarasota*
Berg, Theodore G. - *Niceville*
Browne, Edward J. - *Lady Lake*
Carner, Frank R. SR. - *Holly Hill*
Cason, Charles R. - *Jacksonville*
Crouse, Edward R. - *Freeport*
Erickson, Eustace G. - *Port St. Lucie*
Fay, William S. - *Brandon*
Fitzgerald, Charles A. - *Tampa*
Francess, Robert G. - *Ft. Meyer*
Kane, George W. - *Winter Park*
Kraft, Floyd L. - *Jacksonville*
Lewis, Kenneth A. - *St. Petersburg*
May, Nelson - *Daytona Beach Shores*
Portegay, Richard M. - *North Lauderdale*
Pritchard, Thomas W. - *Palm Bay*
Rhodes, Clarence H. - *Orlando*

Sammon, Bernard J. - *Palm Harbor*
Saxe, Frederick E. - *Hernando*
Schuelke, John T. - *Fort Myers*
Schwartz , Samuel W. - *Ft. Lauderdale*
Sumner, Daniel B. - *Orlando*
Taylor, John D. - *Jacksonville*
Teston, Lonny A. - *Milton*
Thurman Jr., S. R. - *Youngstown*
Trinchitella, William D. - *St. Cloud*
Tuttle Jr., Mcelree - *St. Augustine*
Wetherell, Tom - *Pierson*
Williams, Doctor N. - *Melbourne*
Wilson, Leland D. - *Jacksonville*
Workowski, Howard J. - *Tampa*

Georgia

Ashmore, Wayne - *Carrollton*
Brown, Earl C. - *Atlanta*
Silcox, William L. - *Cumming*

Hawaii

McAbee, John B. - *Aiea*
Mills, George K. - *Lihue*

Iowa

Anderson, Swan O. - *Pochontas*
Carlson, Ralph D. - *Cedar Rapids*
Clow, Edwin J. - *Cherokee*
Eaton, LB Raymond - *Iowa City*
Hedeen, Roy F. - *Lehigh*
Hughes, Clifford C. - *Sioux City*
Leonard, Henry - *Manchester*
Pease, Charles M. - *Shenandoah*
Ruggle, Joseph A. - *Perry*
Sedlacek, Robert A. - *Cedar Rapids*

Spornitz, William E. - *Sioux City*

Idaho

Batt, Seth G. - *Sandpoint*
Krisher, Perry - *Lewiston*
Modrell, Martin J. - *Calder*

Illinois

Chaplin, George - *Round Lake*
Colvin, Ted W. - *East Peoria*
Drew, Marion J. - *McLeansboro*
Dulle, John H. - *Pekin*
Edwards, Thomas A. - *Cottage Hills*
Ehlen, Robert - *Monmouth*
Fogt, Robert L. - *Bolingbrook*
Gleason, Harold I. - *Des Plaines*
Hornsby, Roger D. - *Creve Coeur*
Ivers, Harold W. - *New Baden*
Kleifgen, William J. - *Chicago*
Knowles, Robert W. - *Carlinville*
Kornely, Elmer - *Chicago*
Lang, Robert O. - *Crystal Lake*
Matejovsky, Jerry F. - *Darien*
Ollmann, Harold F. - *Itasca*
Pemberton, Robert L. - *Romeoville*
Perry, Robert J. - *Crystal Lake*
Price, Donald M. - *Lincolnshire*
Rhodes, William R. - *Chicago*
Selke, Carl W. - *Hoffman*
Smith, John F. - *Elgin*
Soma, William N. - *Darien*
Stang, Sr., Leonard J. - *Gurnee*
Switzer, William K. - *Williams Field*
Waymack, Richard G. - *Macomb*
Weiger, Walter J. - *Villa Park*

Indiana

Bruns, Dale E. - *Greensburg*
Diebolt, Edwin J. - *Muncie*
Farmer, Lewis H. - *Economy*
Forecki, Raymond - *Dyer*
Kenter, David L. - *Crawfordsville*
Mitkus, Vito V. - *Carmel*
Morgan, Bruce H. - *Indianapolis*
Reynolds, Robert Wayne - *Speedway*
Simmons, Noel O. - *Indianapolis*
Wilson, Junior T. - *Windfall*

Kansas

Cartwright, Harold - *Osawtomie*
Howard, Darrel - *Wichita*
Miller, George - *Galena*
Schweitzer, George H. - *Manhattan*

Kentucky

Combs, Sidney - *Fisty*
Livesay, Earl T. - *Glasgow*
Mann, Ronald - *Louisville*
Rawlings, Dan K. - *Corbin*

Louisiana

Breaux, Anthony S. - *Huma*
Crow, Bass L. - *Farmerville*
Gaar, Paul V. - *Dodson*
Haase, Charles A. - *Metairie*
Harris, Julius C. - *West Monroe*
Perry Jr., Jessie - *Oakdale*
Sanders, Donald W. - *Lake Charles*

Massachusetts

Benoit, Clifford E. - *Arlington*

Berglund, Bertil T. - *North Easton*

Curewitz, Kenneth E. *Framingham*

Danielson, Edward - *Garner*

Hillman, Frank R. - *W. Springfield*

Mugford, Robert G. - *Sudbury*

Ozelius, E. Gordon - *Plymouth*

Riley, William J. - *Brookline*

Suliman, Ralph H. - *West Boylston*

Maryland

Beair, John L. - *Hagerstown*

Brown, Bernard B. - *Maryland Line*

Frazee, Donovan - *Laurel*

Hodges, Warren D. - *Churchville*

Maddox, Walter L. - *Baltimore*

Reynolds, L. David - *St. Michaels*

Rosier, Melvin K. - *Parkton*

Young, Avery C. - *Laurel*

Maine

Degrass, Howard R. - *Presque Isle*

Falkins, Richard K. - *Brunswick*

Maxwell, John W. - *So. Portland*

Michaud, Lewis - *St. David*

Myers, Irvin - *Bangor*

Smith, Norman L. - *North Yarmouth*

Swanson, Harry D. - *Portland*

Young, Henry F. - *KennebunkPort*

Michigan

Benedict, Lee E. Jr. - *Greenville*

Berg, Spencer B. - *Bloomfield Hills*

Deto , David A. - *Flint*

Drefs, Paul - *Escanoba*

Duty, William Jr. - *Wayne*

Garland, Leslie - *Watervliet*

Hanning, Aaron - *Oscoda*

Holmberg, Chester G. - *Gladstone*

Huntoon, Lyle R. - *Henderson*

Hurst, Jr., Robert J. - *Flushing*

Janes, Robert N. - *New Hudson*

Jury, Harry W. - *East Lansing*

Kies, Marion - *Jonesville*

Law, Donny J. - *Allen Park*

McNett, Wayne A. - *Sanford*

Nickerson, Norman - *Howell*

Ostler, Fred - *Saginaw*

Pollock, Richard L. - *Hudson*

Rathgeb, Lawrence J. - *West Bloomfield*

Russo, Dr. Charles - *Lewiston*

Ryan, Macrice C. - *Linden*

Scott, Jr., William - *Indian River*

Stubelt, Alfred E. - *Benton Harbor*

VerHey, Robert N. - *Holland*

Zobl, Eldred G. - *Bloomfield Hills*

Minnesota

Anda, LeRoy - *Plymouth*

Bendickson, Leland A. - *St. Paul*

Dubbeldee, George - *Marshall*

Goeden, Gerard P. - *Wadena*

Johnson, Odeen C. - *Plymouth*

Moes, Nicholas - *Hastings*

Roberts, Raymond L. - *Vadnais Heights*

Steece, John - *Luverne*

Missouri

Birk , Nelson A. - *Fredericktown*

Brems, Carlton - *St. Louis*

Busdieker, Elwood C. - *Warrenton*

Jameson, J Rex - *King City*

Meyer, Raymond C. - *Sweet Springs*

Nadler, Raymond E. - *Wentzville*
Reineke, Irvin - *Platte City*
Schaefer, Ewald F. - *St. Louis*
Slough, John - *Roach*
Walker, Robert E. - *Macon*

Mississippi
Henry, Wallace L. - Pontotoc

Montana
Dinstel, Dick - *Alzada*
Rigg, Carl F. - *Rudyard*
Sproul, Lewis N. - *Kalispell*

North Carolina
Andrews, James L. - *Wilmington*
Baggerly, Charlie - *Harmony*
Barkley, Gene E. - *Taylorsville*
Causey Sr., Thomas N. - *Greensboro*
Conner, Joseph R. - *Fayetteville*
Hinson, Willie - *Monroe*
Howze, William T. - *Sylva*
Kirkman, Joseph F. - *Greenboro*
Lippard, Richard H. - *Statesville*
McCoy, John J. - *Asheville*
Poole. James L. - *Sparta*
Porter, Samuel H. - *Charlotte*
Settle, James E. - *Hope Mills*
Sherbert, John C. - *Raleigh*
Swain, Ralph L. - *Asheboro*
Wall, Davis E. - *Winston Salem*
Wolfe, Bobby G. - *Davdson*

North Dakota
Furman, Gene F. - *Minot*
Thompson, James R. - *Devils Lake*

Nebraska
Betts, Martin A. - *Bellvue*
Fried, William G. - *Omaha*

Klanderud, Wendell D. - *Blair*
Kohl Jr, Anton F. - *Crete*
Omel, Myron W. - *Aurora*
Strauss, W. A. - *Omaha*
Warner, William A. - *Valparaiso*
Wetovick, August L. - *Fullerton*

New Hampshire
Adame, George T. - *Antrim*
Arel, Lucien - *Claremont*
Baybutt, Richard - *Keene*
Finn, Daniel J. - *Benton*
Parsons, Robert E. - Grantham
Smart Sr., John A. - *Seabrook*
Tilbury, Donald E. - Hampton

New Jersey
Barrentine, Loyd - *Mt. Laurel*
Bollwage, William L. - *Rahway*
Burt, Donald - *Gloucester*
Connelly, Vincent - *Englishtown*
Cooper, Chester L. - *Highland Lakes*
Finan, Norman G. - *Clifton*
Hodge, Robert V. - *Mt. Holly*
Korzen, Peter - *Toms River*
Lambert, Charles J. - *Egg Harbor Town*
Loftus, Andrew J - *Manville*
Long Jr., John P. - *South Hampton*
McKenney, Thomas - *Medford*
Patterson, Donald B. - *Blairstown*
Pollard, Lawrence F. - *Sussex*
Scully, James - *Bayville*
Seavey, William H. - *Browns Mills*
Silva, John D. - *Warren*
Stewart, William J. - *Oakland*
Sutton, Albert - *Lodi*
West, Parker M. - *Hamilton Square*
Koshlap, Eugene - *Toms River*

New Mexico

Schaffner, Jacob - *Albuquerque*

Nevada

Cashman, Donald - *Las Vegas*
Jerdan, John L. - *Las Vegas*
Knight, Richard G. - *Carson City*
Thornton, Valentine - *Reno*

New York

Bartle, Leon - *Webster*
Beacom, Herbert - *Randolph*
Braninghof, Bernard H. - *Troy*
Butler, Floyd C. - *Niagara Falls*
Chamberlain, Wendell - *Belfast*
Cocchieri, Frank P. - *Bronx*
Corhan, Alfred - *Brooklyn*
Covner, George S. - *Flushing*
Debrine, Robert - *Penn Yan*
Demler, Frank E - *Kenmore*
Eastwood, Calvin - *Jackson Heights*
Freeman, Edward H. - *Utica*
Gooch, Hoarce - *Fairport*
Gruber, Victor - *Jamaica*
Howe, Maurice D. - *Endwell*
Huff, Gerald L. - *Churchville*
Kinney, Robert A. - *Penn Yan*
LaBalme, George - *New York*
Liposcak, Frank - *Amagansett*
Lustyk, Joseph E. - *Rochester*
McCoy, Francis E. - *Richfield Springs*
Olshansky, Bernard - *New York*
Owens, William M. - *Niagara Falls*
Panebianco, Thomas - *Roslyn Heights*
Pease, Robert N. - *Peekskill*
Riemer, Wolfgang J. - *Schenectady*
Savaria, Arthur J. - *Cohoes*
Schunzel, Mandred K. - *La Grangeville*
Short, Samuel E. - *Bath*
Slusar, Paul - *West Islip*
Snell, Robert D. - *APO*
Whitley , William - *Long Lake*

Ohio

Boggs, John - *Columbus*
Eick, Richard W. - *Coshocton*
Elliott, Lyman F. - *Toledo*
Everetts, Charles W. - *Columbus*
Friedman, Jerry M. - *Cincinnati*
Frontczak, Thomas A. - *Cleveland*
Guy, Rolland B. - *Mechancsburg*
Kolberg, Howard W - *Canton*
Kraft, Calvin - *Kenton*
Lightcap, Jack D. - *Centerville*
McClusky, Eugene - *Dennison*
Moyer, John G. - *Youngstown*
Rechart, George C. - *Trenton*
Sherman, Justin H. - *Kenton*
Sindeldecker, Lawrence E. - *Powhatan*
Swoyer, Edward H. - *Bellaire*
Ulrich, Joseph M. - *Akron*
Weisend, Donald J. - *Rootstown*
Wem, Robert - *Youngstown*

Oklahoma

Barnes, Ray - *Oklahoma City*
Bowers, Billie H. - *Idabel*
Dennis, Arvy - *Shawnee*
Kirby, Fred H. - *Oklahoma City*
Melton, Henry L. - *Grove*
Plummer, Alexander C. - *Tonkawa*
Rickman, Orrin R. - *Moore*
Shepherd, George D. - *Stillwater*

Thomas, James L. - *Sapulpa*
VanCuren, John - *Tulsa*

Oregon

Barraclough, Rodney - *Mulino*
Coulson, Anthony - *Bandon*
Doherty, Kenneth R. - *Pendelton*
Ducich, John - *Sunriver*
Ellenwood, Robert A. - *Roseburg*
Kyte, William A. - *Lebanon*
Lovelace, Tyrus R. - *Eugene*
Martin, Raymond E. - *King City*
O'Connor, Edmond B. - *Merrill*
Porter, Thomas G. - *Albany*
Sherwood, Edwyn R. - *Brookings*
Waldron, Orlando Kline - *Salem*

Pennsylvania

Altman, William H. - *Oakmont*
Berry, Gerald E. - *Philadelphia*
Bokus , Len - *Northampton*
Bovius, Leonard - *Allentown*
Cramer, Charles E. - *Greensburg*
Dagutis, Donald J. - *Colmar*
Dray, Paul R. - *Eldred*
English, Robert E. - *Erie*
Facemyer, Charles - *Latrobe*
Fesovich, Pete - *Britol*
Flower, George L. - *Lower Gaynear*
George, Glenn C. - *Kittanning*
Gutacker, Jr., Harry C. - *Columbia*
Hemrick, Harold E. - *Lewisburg*
Johnson, Harold E. - *Bedford*
Kirkpatrick, George H. - *Charleroi*
Kokoski, Thaddeus, *Moon Township*
Kuehn, Charles E. - *Lehighton*

Lacombe, Joseph - *Milroy*
Ludwick, Richard - *Delmont*
Lynn, David - *Freeport*
Malarkey, William F. - *West*

Wyoming

Mills Jr., Clyde D. - *Butler*
Naccari, Edward R. - *King of Prussia*
Osborne, Allan B. - *Etters*
Popp, Joseph P. - *Philadelphia*
Shoup, Albert - *St. Marys*
Slack, Alfred L. - *Harrisburg*
Strunk, Thomas E. - *Williamsport*
Student, David - *King of Prussia*
Turner, Mahlon M. - *Walnutport*
Webb II, Charles J. - *Philadelphia*
Wisnewski, Edward - *Folsom*

South Carolina

Downey, Robert J. - *Little River*
Eddy Jr., Alfred K. - *Salem*
Lee, Jamie L. - *Bennetsville*
Rauscher, Walter M. - *Port Royal*
Smith, Cletis H. - *Chapin*

South Dakota

Adney, William J. - *Selby*

Tennessee

Conyers, J C R - *Goodlettsville*
Grandy, Ralph Q. - *McMinnville*
Hunter, Robert E. - *Townsend*
Jernigan, Ben W. - *Sweetwater*
McCall, William E. - *Knoxville*
Waldo, Frank E. - *Kingsport*
Weaver, James G. - *Alamo*

Young, William T. - *Arlington*

Texas

Bennett, Hoyt H. - *Hurst*
Braden, James E. - *San Marcos*
Campbell, Jimmie D - *Mabank*
Cloyd, James O. - *Dallas*
Coli, Raymond R. - *El Paso*
Craig, James - *Everman*
Davidson, Billie A. - *Arlington*
Duckworth, George U. - *El Paso*
Ellis, Garvin B. - *Centerville*
Farley, William E. - *Baytown*
Harrell, Max - *Brownwood*
Haynes, Robert L. - *Humble*
Helleson, Troy P. - *Waco*
Horton, Jr., H. Hollis - *Friona*
Jameson, Donald W. - *Pasadena*
Jones, James A. - *Houston*
Laws, Seybert L. - *Delvalle*
Matera, John - *Dallas*
Morgan, William E. - *Katy*
Nitsch, Earl J. - *Brenham*
Olson , Fred - *Marble Falls*
Raabe, Howard J. - *Weimar*
Roberts, Henry C. - *Arlington*
Roberts, Thane - *Amarillo*
Rumpf, Darrell R. - *San Antonio*
Russell, James O. - *Terrell*
Shaw, Douglas W. - *Amarillio*
Stansberry, Robert R. - *Seguin*
Webster, Wilbur R. - *El Paso*
Williams, John W. - *Killeen*
Yehnert, Robert J. - *Richardson*

Utah

Lutz, Fredrick - *Ogden*
Miner, Bert D. - *Springville*

Virginia

Bell, Millard C. - *Newport News*
Belote, Robert P. - *Leesburg*
Bighouse, Edmond J. - *Hamilton*
Daly, David J. - *Newport News*
Diehl, Jacob C. - *Staunton*
Marshall, Orval A. - *Manassas*
Ommert, Charles R. - *Arlington*
Piggott, Albert - *Petersburg*
Puckett, Glenn R. - *Dungannon*
Racey, Rodney L. - *Strasburg*

Vermont

Reed, Otis - *Brattleboro*

Washington

Anderson, Phillip - *Spokane*
Christianson, Robert J. - *Seattle*
Eames, Aerial - *East Wenatchee*
Gangl, Carl F. - *Yakima*
Keller, Charles E. - *Marysville*
Krous, George R. - *Spokane*
Lanning, Willard J. - *Pasco*
Lewis, Donald - *Spokane*
Richards, Raymond H. - *Seattle*
Sanders, Duane V. - *Newport*
Tsuchida, Kiwamu - *Kirkland*
Zurfluh, Thomas R. - *Tacoma*

Wisconsin

Biles, Everett S. - *Durand*
Conway, Dr. Richard W. - *Edgerton*
Dascenzo, Robert - *Pewaukee*
Fischer, Lawrence F. - *Muskego*
Haines DVM, John M. - *Athens*
Kilday, Douglas R. - *Oshkosh*
Lightner, Corliss A. - *Oconto*

Martin, Cyril B. - *Hancock*
Martin, Ralph G. - *Fond Du Lac*
Nelson, Donald M. - *Ellsworth*
Olivier, Edward A. - *Menomonee Falls*
Plouff, Herbert J. - *Pewaukee*
Rasch, Jacob - *Kenosha*
Shinabarger, Robert - *Beloit*
Wagner, Clarence J. - *Chilton*

West Virginia
Benda, David P. - *Hedgesville*
Casto, G.N. - *Bartow*
Fisher, Joseph - *Montgomery*

Lough, Leonard - *Jacksonburg*
Sendling, Donald L. - *Clarksburg*

Canada
Lindquist, Arthur D. - *Vancouver, BC*

Japan
Leidy, George D. - *Ginowan City*
*Ishikawa, Tatsumi - *Toyko*
*Morota, Suguru - *Toyko*

*Honorary member, served as staff worker at the American Embassy for the Honor Guard.

BIBLIOGRAPHY

Ambrose, Stephen E. <u>Duty, Honor, Country: A History of West Point</u>. Baltimore: Johns Hopkins Press, 1966.

Chen, Jian. <u>China's Road to the Korean War: The Making of the Sino-American Confrontation</u>. New York: Columbia University Press, 1994.

Cohen, Theodore. <u>Remaking Japan: The American Occupation as New Deal</u>. New York: Free Press, 1987.

Dower, John W. <u>Embracing Defeat: Japan in the Wake of World War II</u>. New York: W. W. Norton and The New Press, 1999.

Dower, John. <u>War without Mercy: Race and Power in the Pacific War</u>. New York: Random House, 1987.

Eichelberger, Robert L. <u>Dear Miss Em: General</u>

<u>Eichelberger's War in the Pacific, 1942-1945</u>. Westport, Connecticut: Greenwood Press, 1972.

Finn, Richard B. <u>Winners in Peace: MacArthur, Yoshida, and Postwar Japan</u>. Berkeley: University of California Press, 1992.

Goulden, Joseph C. <u>Korea: The Untold Story of the War</u>. New York: Times Books, 1982.

Harach, Joseph C. <u>At the Hinge of History: A Reporter's Story</u>. Athens, Georgia: University of Georgia Press, 1993.

Hunt, Frazier. <u>The Untold Story of Douglas MacArthur</u>. New York: Devin-Adair Co., 1954.

James, D. Clayton. <u>The Years of MacArthur: Volume I, 1880-1941</u>. Boston: Houghton Mifflin, 1970.

James, D. Clayton. <u>The Years of MacArthur: Volume II, 1941-1945.</u> Boston: Houghton Mifflin, 1975.

James, D. Clayton. <u>The Years of MacArthur: Volume Ill, 1945-1964</u>. Boston: Houghton Mifflin, 1985.

Karnow, Stanley. <u>In Our Image: America's Empire in the Philippines</u>. New York: Random House, 1989.

Kase, Toshikazu. <u>Journey to the Missouri</u>. New Haven: Yale University Press, 1950.

Knox, Donald. <u>Death March: The Survivors of Bataan</u>. New York: Harcourt Brace Jovanovich, 1981.

Larrabee, Eric. <u>Commander in Chief: FDR, His Lieutenants, and Their War</u>. New York: Simon & Schuster Inc., 1988.

Leary, William, ed. <u>We Shall Return: MacArthur's Commanders and the Defeat of Japan 1942-1945</u>. Lexington: University Press of Kentucky, 1988.

Lee, Clark and Richard Henschel. <u>Douglas MacArthur</u>. New York: Holt, 1952.

MacArthur, Douglas. <u>Reminiscences: Douglas MacArthur, General of the Army</u>. New York: McGraw-Hill Book Company, 1964.

Manchester, William. <u>American Caesar: Douglas MacArthur, 1880-1964</u>. New York: Dell Publishing, 1978.

McCullough, David. <u>Truman</u>. New York: Simon and Schuster, 1992.

Perret, Geoffrey. <u>Old Soldiers Never Die: The Life of Douglas MacArthur</u>. New York: Random House, 1996

Petillo, Carol. <u>Douglas MacArthur: The Philippine Years</u>. Bloomington: Indiana University Press, 1981.

Pogue, Forrest. <u>George C. Marshall, V.11: Ordeal and Hope, 1939-1942</u>. New York: Viking Press, n.d.

Pogue, Forrest. <u>George C. Marshall, V. Ill: Organizer of Victory, 1943-1945</u>. New York: Viking Press, n.d.

Quezon, Manuel L. <u>The Good Fight</u>. New York: D. Appleton-Century Company, Inc., 1946.

Reilly, Henry J. <u>Americans All: The Rainbow at War</u>. Columbus, Ohio: F.J. Heer Printing Co., 1936.

Romulo, Carlos P. <u>Last Man Off Bataan</u>. London: Sphere, 1969.

Rovere, Richard and Arthur Schlesinger, Jr. <u>General MacArthur and President Truman: The Struggle for Control of American Foreign Policy</u>. New Brunswick: Transaction Publishers, 1992.

Schaller, Michael. <u>The American Occupation of Japan</u>. New York: Oxford University Press, 1985.

Schailer, Michael. Douglas MacArthur: The Far Eastern General. New York: Oxford University Press, 1989.

Spector, Ronald. Eagle Against the Sun: The American War with Japan. New York: Vintage, 1985.

Stoler, Mark A. George C. Marshall: Soldier-Statesman of the American Century. Boston: Twayne Publishers, 1989.

Taaffe, Stephen R. MacArthur's Jungle War: The 1944 New Guinea Campaign. Lawrence, Kansas: University Press of Kansas, 1998.

Truman, Harry S. Memoirs, Vol.11: Years of Trial and Hope. Garden City, N.Y.: Doubleday, 1956.

Yoshida, Shigeru. The Yoshida Memoirs. Boston: Houghton Mifflin Company, 1962.

Young, Kenneth Ray. The General's General: The Life and Times of Arthur MacArthur. Boulder: Westview Press, 1994.

BOOK ORDER FORM

Gaijin Shogun

General Douglas MacArthur
Stepfather of Postwar Japan

Name_____

Address_____

City_____State_____Zip_____

Postal Orders:

_____copies at $14.95 each_____

Shipping & handling (U.S.) $1.50/bk_____

Shipping & handling (Int'l) $5.00/bk_____

Calif. residents add $1.20/book sales tax_____

Total _____

Send check or money order payable to

The Sektor Company
Post Office Box 501005
San Diego, Ca 92150

Orders filled within 1-2 weeks

Comments about the book:

_____

_____

_____

_____

_____

BOOK ORDER FORM

Gaijin Shogun

General Douglas MacArthur
Stepfather of Postwar Japan

Name _____

Address _____

City_____State_____Zip_____

Postal Orders:

_____copies at $14.95 each_____

Shipping & handling (U.S.) $1.50/bk_____

Shipping & handling (Int'l) $5.00/bk_____

Calif. residents add $1.20/book sales tax_____

Total _____

Send check or money order payable to

The Sektor Company
Post Office Box 501005
San Diego, Ca 92150

Orders filled within 1-2 weeks

Comments about the book:

_____
_____
_____
_____
_____
_____